Three Plays

Books by JOYCE CAROL OATES

NOVELS

Bellefleur
Cybele
Unholy Loves
Son of the Morning
Childwold
The Assassins
Do With Me What You Will
Wonderland
them
Expensive People
A Garden of Earthly Delights
With Shuddering Fall

SHORT STORIES

All the Good People I've Left Behind
Night-Side
Crossing the Border
The Goddess and Other Women
Marriages and Infidelities
The Wheel of Love
Upon the Sweeping Flood
By the North Gate
The Hungry Ghosts
The Seduction
The Poisoned Kiss, Fernandes/Oates

CRITICISM

New Heaven, New Earth:
  The Visionary Experience in Literature
The Edge of Impossibility:
  Tragic Forms in Literature

PLAYS

Three Plays

POEMS

Anonymous Sins
Love and Its Derangements
Angel Fire
The Fabulous Beasts
Women Whose Lives Are Food, Men Whose Lives Are Money

Three Plays

by

Joyce Carol Oates

ONTOLOGICAL PROOF OF MY EXISTENCE

MIRACLE PLAY

THE TRIUMPH OF THE SPIDER MONKEY

THE ONTARIO REVIEW PRESS
Princeton, New Jersey

ACKNOWLEDGEMENTS

Ontological Proof of My Existence was first published in *Partisan Review*, Vol. 37, October, 1970.
Miracle Play was first published by Black Sparrow Press, Los Angeles, California, 1974.

CAUTION: Professionals and amateurs are hereby warned that *Ontological Proof of My Existence, Miracle Play,* and *The Triumph of the Spider Monkey* are fully protected under the Universal Copyright Convention and the International Copyright Union, and are subject to royalty. All rights, including professional, amateur, motion picture, recitation, lecturing, public reading, radio and television broadcasting, and the rights of translation into foreign languages are strictly reserved. All inquiries should be addressed to Blanche C. Gregory, Inc., 2 Tudor Place, New York, N.Y. 10017.

© 1980 Joyce Carol Oates
Manufactured in the United States of America

Cover: "Cat-burglar in Bologna," Anon. c. 1925, *Wide World Photo*

Library of Congress Cataloging in Publication Data

Oates, Joyce Carol, 1938-
  Three plays.

  CONTENTS: Ontological proof of my existence.—
Miracle play.—The triumph of the spider monkey.
  I. Title
PS3565.A8T5   812'.54   80-20210
ISBN 0-86538-001-5
ISBN 0-86538-002-3 (pbk.)

Distributed by **PERSEA BOOKS,** Inc.
225 Lafayette Street
New York, N.Y. 10012

CONTENTS

PREFACE

Ceremony, ritual: the inexpressible coherence of 'fate': the dishar-
monious music that is torn from us at certain moments in our lives,
and in history—these are the elements that underlie drama. Atop them
nearly anything can be imagined and played, depending upon the
courage of the individual voices.

My fascination with the drama is a fascination with its oldest, and
in a way most conservative function: the mimesis of an action 'tragic'
in its intensity, involving defeat and triumph, often in inexpressible
terms. Language does not always fail—it quite frequently succeeds—
but images must never fail. The gesture will outlive its moment in
the plot.

The basic 'texts' of the plays are surrealist, and their mode of
discourse poetry. Consequently a surface realism and a prose facade
may be employed for as long as the director thinks effective. Movement
is always from prose to poetry, from 'realism' to 'surrealism,' but the
ease with which the metamorphosis is accomplished in each play (and
in scenes within each play) must be determined in part by the sophisti-
cation of the audience. The more sophisticated the audience, the more
readily one can dispose with a 'professional' slickness and reveal, even
allude to, the ceremonial underpinnings of the story. Peter V. of
Ontological Proof of My Existence has all our names in his book.

The plays are clearly meant to be formal rituals of sacrifice, on
their most fundamental (and secret) level. Strong actors might convey
the struggle almost physically—as in fact I have seen them convey it,
through facial and bodily gestures that are improvised. The tug-of-war
is not simply for triumph of a kind but for survival itself in the on-
going drama. To be less than the star is to be—obliterated.

It is helpful for the actors to imagine themselves performing on two planes, as we 'perform' in real life. We sense ourselves more or less contained within a coherent structure, a 'story' that is being told (without a storyteller?)—we are *characters* experienced in the third-person. At the same time we cannot help but transcend the story inter-mittently, suffering glimpses of its gravity, its momentum (though we can do very little to alter its plot). We are, consequently, characters in an anarchic prose poem that is plotless and timeless and has been experienced throughout human history. Our mode of discourse for the one is prose, for the other, poetry.

Though these are highly self-conscious plays their 'realism' should not be scorned. Imagine simply that the function of the Greek chorus has been absorbed into the participants of the drama—perhaps into the texture of the drama itself. Action and commentary; commentary and action; analysis; illumination; stasis; and then movement once again. The plays' secret passage is from prose to poetry, from a time-locked 'story' to anarchy. My faith that this corresponds to our own secret passages—as speakers of prose, as speakers of poetry—is absolute.

Ritual is always stylized and impersonal; that is why it is ritual, why it is both terrible and necessary. Life may not be a constant struggle for self-definition but its crucial moments are, and drama focuses upon those crucial moments. Drama is greedy, insatiable: it swallows up great expanses of 'ordinary life': not to dismiss them but to transform them. The more abstract the drama, the more rigorously its discourse may correspond to the secrets of 'ordinary life.' Perfect gestures outlive the plots that surround them and make them possible.

Ceremony, ritual, sacrifice. And a final illumination. These are conservative elements. In a drama that takes itself so seriously, with such self-conscious gravity, moments of sheer comedy—comedy that is free, even, of parody—are irresistible. The more comic the struggle for survival is imagined, the more compelling the play: up to a point. But of course that point cannot be passed or the ritual is destroyed.

Shelley of *Ontological Proof of My Existence* begins her play strongly and even defiantly; but she loses it, as she loses the audience, to the superior imagination—the strength and bravado—of her enter-prising lover Peter V. In *Miracle Play* everyone contends for victory, simply because victory—however minimal—assures the only possible conditions for survival. Titus, like Peter, is an industrious entrepeneur: he cannot be defeated since he is, in his glory, the Savior of his society's secret religion. The 'miracle' is not that Titus succeeds at murder, and will not be stopped; the 'miracle' is far more basic—that he dares to define himself as if he might be, indeed, self-born, self-generated. Both

Peter V. and Titus are mock-saviors and mock-playwrights whose refusal to be mere third-person characters assures them victory.

The Triumph of the Spider Monkey, the most recent of the plays, and for obvious reasons the play closest to my heart, involves a 'tragic' hero who is both criminal and victim: one who acquiesces finally to his fate, which he has tried to misread as destiny. Bobbie Gotteson's story has evolved through so many stages in my writing career that its basic meaning has become inescapable to me, yet no less painful for being self-evident. The thwarted artist, the mocked and ridiculed and doomed artist, the artist who is tirelessly (and madly) convinced of his genius—how has it come about that he is, in the public's rapt eye, merely another mass murderer?—merely the 'most appealing' of recent mass murderers in the great State of California? And how has it come about that his pursuit of his obsession has involved the deaths of others? They are innocent deaths as well—as Bobbie admits freely, "They were all innocent." Yet the Spider Monkey is redeemed—in a manner of speaking. His passion is a triumph: in a manner of speaking.

I have imagined these plays as rites of sacrifice, then: but they are also, and more obviously, arenas in which warring and harmonious voices take on life. The 'voices' are those of strangers—yet, to the playwright, they have a curious mesmerizing resonance. No form of art is perhaps so graphically autobiographical in essence—in emotional essence—as the drama; yet no form of art can appear so distant, so detached from its imaginative source. The 'voices' become those of actors: the sensibility of the playwright becomes that of the director: the original play is seen not to exist, except as a tissue of words, awaiting life. As a writer, as one who believes in the relative permanence of the written word, I find both astonishing and saddening the fact that actors' performances are largely lost. The inspired moments, the half-conscious gestures that are so perfect, and so fleeting—the uncanny ability of the good actor to submerge himself in his role—the extraordinary subtlety of actors as they play together: it seems to me tragic that these precious achievements are fated to be lost, except in memory. (And what is memory? Where does it reside?) Consequently it seems to me that drama's most instinctive curve is toward the tragic, or even more violently toward the ironic and the parodistic. In Bobbie Gotteson's words, the music of the drama, and perhaps of all art, is simply a way of trying to disguise something so humanly sad it can't be expressed in any other terms.

Joyce Carol Oates
Princeton, New Jersey

ONTOLOGICAL PROOF OF MY EXISTENCE

for
Maurice Edwards

Ontological Proof of My Existence was first performed at the Cubiculo Theatre, 414 West 51 Street, New York City, on February 3, 1972. The cast was as follows:

Shelley ....,..................................... Eileen Dietz

Peter V. .... Ray Cole

Father .... Jess Adkins

Martin Raven .... Dan Lutzky

Directed by Maurice Edwards

CHARACTERS:

Shelley, a girl of about sixteen

Peter V., a man of indeterminate age

Shelley's Father, a man in his forties

Martin Raven, a man in his thirties

What are the proofs of God?
—a question frequently posed in past centuries: but no longer.
What are the proofs of man?
—a question more reasonably posed for our time.

Lights up, slowly. A room with a high ceiling; unpainted brick walls; unfurnished and yet cluttered; desolate; inhuman; on the edge of nowhere. Yet comfortable, lived-in. A curiously domestic hovel. A window, stage right. A door, stage left. A mattress on the floor stage right.

SHELLEY *is lying immobile on the mattress, beneath a filthy blanket. The lights continue to come up: cold, impersonal, dreamlike. There is something unreal about the lighting as well as the setting, as if the play were taking place at the lowest level of human vitality, at the point at which the human passes subtly and unprotestingly into the unhuman.*

SHELLEY *wakes. She comes gradually to life — to consciousness. One must feel the difficulty, the struggle. To come back! To come back — again! She is exhausted, drugged, groggy: she shakes her head, trying to clear her thoughts. At first it isn't clear whether she is a boy or a girl — she is extremely thin, with very short clipped hair, a face that is neuter, innocent, blank, raw. (SHELLEY's face is important, as we shall see. She must possess, beneath her apparent face, one of a curious stubborn strength, hard-boned, even defiant. For — from a certain angle — SHELLEY is the strongest personality in this drama.)*

SHELLEY *gets to her feet with difficulty. She is wearing jeans and a boy's T-shirt with nothing beneath it. She is barefoot, or in dirty socks. At first her manner is groggy and whining; then she becomes excited, manic. There is an unfocussed, restless, jerky quality to her movements.*

SHELLEY: In the next hour they are going to prove that I exist.... (*in a clearer voice*) In the next hour they are going to prove that I exist! The proof will be shown to me! Demonstrated here on this stage! For I am a laboratory experiment.... I submit, I don't resist. (*approaching the stage apron, slightly mocking*) I am the girl whose body is found in a vacant lot, beneath a pile of rubble...or in a jail cell...where I've hanged myself, out of spite for the matron who wouldn't give me cigarettes. Sometimes I am found in condemned buildings like this one: in rooms with high ceilings, bare floors, exposed pipes, a single stained mattress on the floor. You give me a single column on page seventeen of the newspaper and then you turn the page...for...after all.... (*yawning*) After all there is page eighteen to be read. (*a pause, then briskly*) This is an era of proofs! Scientists have proven a great deal! The sun has been proven to be a perfectly ordinary star with a diameter of 1,392,000 kilometers lying at an average distance of 149,600,000 kilometers from the earth...it will continue to shine so brightly and cheerily for another 5,000 million years before exploding and swallowing us all up. Solar systems have been discovered in the cavities of our back molars...great kingdoms in our chromosomes ...of which we know nothing. Television proves that many people exist: you switch them on, you switch them off: it's electricity: it's—*easy*. God exists—God can be found in the dictionary and in the old chronicles. Slaps, kicks, love-maulings, a fistful of your hair pulled from your head—these are proofs that other people exist. You'll see them. You'll feel them. Do they hurt? Oh yes! Yes. (*pause*) My head was banged on the floor over there (*pointing to a corner of the stage*) and it made me understand that the floor exists. One day I got very tall and the ceiling up there (*pointing to the ceiling*) brushed against the top of my head, so I knew that the ceiling existed also. I'm hungry.

(SHELLEY *walks slowly about the stage, in a daze, looking for something to eat.*)

SHELLEY: There's food in here somewhere. Where did he put it? I think I smell food. Is it under here? (*lifting some junk*) My head aches. I think it's because I haven't eaten. I ate the day before yesterday, but what about yesterday? I made my husband, Martin, something to eat yesterday, or maybe it was the day before yesterday. I wonder if he ate all of it, or did he leave some? Where is it? My head aches but I'm not really hungry. My stomach is very tight and probably food couldn't squeeze into it. I don't like the smell in here. Too many people have lived in here. Now the building is condemned, I overheard Peter telling Martin that, I think I overheard him saying that.... Where is Peter? He hasn't been up here for three days. I need Peter. He should return in the next hour. Peter can hold back all this crowd, all these people. He understands. I need him, I need medicine from him, help from him, I am in love with him and he gives me love. Sometimes he presses me flat against the floor, right against the floor, so that I can't move. Then he breaths into me.... My head aches. I can't see right. Are the corners of this room fixed right? (*pause*) The people who will come in this room are: Peter V., my lover; my father, who is hurrying here now; and another man who is a mystery, Martin Raven, my new husband. Three men, and myself. There is a crowd of men around me. (*She brushes at her hair with her hands, quickly, coquettishly.*) I wonder if I'm still pretty? Peter forgot to bring a mirror up. He said he would, then he forgot. I have been in this room for a long time now; I don't go out. They don't let me out. I would hurt myself outside on the street, anyway...someone would find me. I don't think the door there is locked, but Peter V. told me never to leave and so I can't leave. He gave me absolute instructions ten days ago, or a month ago. I don't remember. If he hadn't forbidden me to leave I think I would leave...I'm hungry, I think I would leave...I would walk over to the door, (*She walks to the door.*) I would see if I could open it...(*She opens the door, which is not locked.*) and if it was unlocked I would leave. But it's locked. It's been locked for a month now. I can't get out.

(SHELLEY *stands at the door, gazing out abstractedly. She speaks in a sing-song, monotonous voice, which gradually becomes more animated, more excited.*)

SHELLEY: Outside this door there is a corridor. The plaster is falling down. I can see the top of a stairway. There are doors along the corridor—some of them are open. Some are closed. Listen!—is that someone crying? (*She listens. No sound.*) I think there are many people in this building besides myself. I heard some girls giggling last night. Little girls. There are thuds, screams, long monotonous arguments, radios, televisions, footsteps.... This is Peter's building and he can populate it the way he wants. He loves many girls, not just me. I know this. I'm not jealous. I'm not certain of my body (*She touches herself vaguely.*) so how can I be jealous? How can I be jealous of what he does to other bodies in this building? I wish Peter would come back. I need him. And my father, I know that my father is on his way, yes, he's on his way, and my new husband Martin is on his way, they are all drawing together, coming together in this room, in me, a crowd of men coming together inside me.... I wish Peter would get here first! I wish everything would speed up, my life speed up, the beating in my head get faster, faster, so that I could be shown how I exist the way you are all certain that you exist....

(SHELLEY *walks slowly to the left of the stage. Peter V. appears in the doorway and enters, silently. He is anywhere from twenty-five to forty years old. His clothes are rakish and jaunty, expensive. An ascot, white shoes. Friendly, sinister. He will contend with* SHELLEY *for the audience's sympathy.*)

SHELLEY: (*at the window*) I wish you could see out this window! Streets converge ... crowds ... listen to that traffic! This must be the center of the world where all the winds rush together. (*softly*) There is a building across the street exactly like this building. Perhaps it is a mirror-image? And I see a mirror-Shelley at one of the windows, looking out. Most of the windows are boarded up ... that building is condemned too, like this one ... another Peter owns it ... or maybe it is my Peter, my lover. (*She waves, hesitantly.*) Oh but she isn't waving back! Just a face ... a very pale face ... big eyes ... eyes set deep in their sockets.... She isn't cute, like me. He wouldn't love *her*.

PETER: (*fondly, contemptuously*) The very first night I brought her here, she acted exactly like that! Always posing ... showing off ... primping and preening ... as if before an audience ... an audience of *very interested* and *sympathetic* people. The way girls do ... it's so American ... so cute ... a curse, so cute. Girls are—well, so cute! You can shake them until their eyes roll back in their skulls, you can hug them until their ribs crack, you can knock their pretty front teeth out ... and still they're posing for you, anxious and hopeful, sweet little things, their underarms shaved hairless and innocent—a sign of great virtue. Right? Cute as cheerleaders. In fact, many of them have been cheerleaders—several, among my wide acquaintance. And Shelley too. Is Shelley her name? Shelley. Yes. My Shelley. Observe her: after forty-five days of this she's still ready to break into a cheer, to jump up and stretch her shapely little body, leading our team to victory ... and all that. (PETER *is speaking zestfully, as if promoting goods; but* SHELLEY *slouches wearily.)*

SHELLEY: That first night I ran to the window here, I pushed at the glass.... Did I want to jump out the window? It's five stories to the sidewalk. Or did I want to scare him? (*giggling*) My new boy friend! ... I wonder how I looked. My hair was long then, my skin was clear, I know I was pretty. All girls my age are pretty, more or less. We can't help it. I can remember pushing at the window... standing here ... my long hair ... people out on the street ... late Saturday afternoon and lots of people ... the smells of food from the street ... I wanted to push the window apart so that people could see me up here. I wanted to cry out to them, "Look, it's me, it's Shelley, I've come to live here with you, I'm going to be one of you! I'm in love!" Peter V. came up behind me and put his arms around me. Oh, he loved me then, he loved me for a week or more ... he told me it was the longest he'd ever loved anyone....

PETER: A girl of sixteen or seventeen, like that girl, is irresistible. Even if you've been out on business for three days, as I have ... three days straight with only a few hours sleep, collecting fees, paying people off, making telephone calls, in and out of taxis and in and out of buildings — what a life! I know too many people. Too many girls like this one. Still, she's irresistible, isn't she? Look at her healthy gleaming hair, look at her healthy body! The very heartland of America is between her ribs, I promise you. Her legs are pearly and long and lovely. About her there is only the odor of talcolm powder and corn flakes — nothing more, I promise you! The Girl Scout insignia is tattooed on her breast. I promise all that, and more.

SHELLEY: I thought I was calling out for people down there to see me so that they would be jealous. After all, Peter had picked me! But now I think I was calling for help. He had the door locked already. I couldn't get out. He locked the door first, then pressed me flat on the floor — not on the mattress, it wasn't in here yet. He kept banging my head against the floor, making love to me. He convinced me that I didn't exist. My body broke up into pieces, in his hands. It's all different pieces.

PETER: (*enthusiastically*) Is she trying to break the window? Trying to jump out? I'm not going to let her, not yet. Look at the spirit she has! What muscles! What a lovely girl, eh? How much is she worth to you? She has held up very well, it must have been her excellent

family life back home, the good dental care and the fortified cereal
and the fuzzy lined boots; she is from an excellent suburb of one of
our great American cities. Great care went into her making,
centuries of care. She's a Midwestern beauty. Look, she's preening,
she's posing for us out of sheer exuberance! (SHELLEY *stands
without moving, staring down into the street.*)

SHELLEY (*turning blindly, not seeing* PETER) He broke my body up into
pieces. I am like a jigsaw puzzle. It was right here, on the floor...
this spot here.... But there's no mark. There's no blood. People
get nailed to the floor and bleed to death and there is no mark to
show what they went through, no evidence, no proof of their
existence.... The world is crowded with invisible people who can't
prove that they exist. (*lightly, lyrically*) Anyway, he loved me! He
might love me again! Peter, you did love me!

(*She runs to* PETER *and extends her arms, still without quite seeing
him.* PETER *eludes her, like a dancer. He makes a gesture to the
audience, grinning, as if exhibiting the girl, a possession of his.*)

SHELLEY: I got on a bus and got off a bus, and there I was outside, a few
yards away from here, on a Saturday afternoon. What a crowd! All
those happy people! I could smell food—hotdogs, mustard, pizza
—I ran along the sidewalk with my coat flapping open around me,
my skirt very short, my legs very pretty in bright blue stockings,
like legs seen flashing through water— And you came up behind
me, Peter, and put your arms around me—

PETER: I stood on the sidewalk and watched you run up to me. What a
lovely little girl! If I closed my eyes slightly you turned into a herd
of lovely little girls!—a herd, and all so cute! Your hair was very
long then, in the style of your suburb, well-brushed and healthy, a
golden brown. Your yellow coat flapped open to show your cute
little body and your busy little legs, in blue stockings. I was like a
light-house, I stood in the crowd and you saw me.

SHELLEY: You took my arm....

PETER: You grabbed my arm.

SHELLEY: My fingers closed about your arm by themselves... I clutched
at you, I was falling, drowning, I couldn't keep my balance.... I
felt so weak... I didn't know where I was.... I grabbed your arm
and everything seemed to fall toward you. The sidewalk tilted

toward you. Gravity began. (*She poses prettily.*) I got off the bus and there you were! You were what I had been promised. I dreamt about you or someone like you. Two times before I had run away from home, but I never found you.... Never. Only police matrons, women with coarse tired skin, cigarette breath, sour and ironic from years of doing good deeds....

PETER: What was I wearing?

SHELLEY: Something white—with green stripes—a green necktie—a straw hat—sunglasses—white shoes— You were so handsome! Your teeth were so white! Your hair was curly, like wood-shavings, stiff and curly and bunched up around your hat! My hand went out to you and my fingers closed about your arm, grasping your arm—

PETER: I saw that you were 5 foot 4 inches, that you weighed 115 pounds, that you were 16 years old, out for a holiday and needing someone to protect you. Your eyes were hazy even then—such pretty blue eyes!—tiny circles radiated out from the iris, looking so blind, so trusting, so much in love. You wanted me to explain to you that you didn't exist, that it wasn't your fault and you were not to blame and nobody would punish you—so I took you home.

SHELLEY: (*turning away suddenly*) You kept bumping my head against the floor. It was the first time for me. You didn't listen. I had to come all those miles on the bus to get away from home, to find someone to love, it was the first time for me, but you didn't listen. Oh, everything entered me! It came into me! The pavement outside —the crowds—the traffic—the buildings—the windows—the doors—the roofs— Everything entered my body, flooding into me. You were like a light-house—the beacon on a light-house! That light! That beam of light! My body broke. It flowed out into the city. It came apart into pieces. (*She touches her body, as if in a daze; she looks down at herself.*) There is a body here. I know that. And I am thinking, I am speaking, out of a skull that is on top of this body, covered with flesh, a living skull, the bone hidden from sight. I know this. But there is no connection between myself and this body. I could go on talking and my voice could float away, into the clouds... I am the size of an angel, the size of a fingernail ...I could be borne into the sky on a piece of soot, a piece of charred paper flying in the air.... (*suddenly, frightened*) Peter is coming! I can hear him coming!

(SHELLEY *throws herself down on the mattress.* PETER *leaves the doorway and returns again, rapping on the door. He claps his hands. His tone is louder, even more hearty, slightly scolding.*)

PETER: (*playfully*) What the hell? What? Wake up, little girl! Get up! Don't you know it's five o'clock in the afternoon, it's time for you to be fixing the house, cleaning and polishing and cooking, don't you know your husband will be home in half an hour?

SHELLEY: (*pretends to be waking*) My head aches . . . what happened . . . ? I don't feel right. . . .

PETER: You were lying in that same position when I left three days ago. Shame on you, how lazy you are! For shame! What will your husband say? Do you want to anger him again? Why isn't supper on the stove?

SHELLEY: I can't make myself sit up . . . my head aches . . . I feel sick. . . .

PETER: Up, up! (*clapping his hands*) For shame! Have you been hoarding those little white pills? Has someone rolled pills under the door to you? Have you made friends with another little girl, are you rapping on the walls in a secret code? You know you're forbidden to communicate with anyone.

SHELLEY: Yes. . . .

PETER: Then wake up, get going! (*pulls her to her feet in a parody of a dance routine—lightly, musically*) First make the bed. Yes, like that. Yes. Tidy up the house. Yes. This is fine. (*looking about at the mess*) This is what he's paying for, after all. Domestic life. But you'd better start supper right away so that he can smell it when he climbs the stairs. That's important. He needs to smell supper cooking when he climbs the stairs. He works all day and thinks of this time—smelling supper as he climbs the stairs, dreaming of you, his head filled with you— (*seizing her and walking her back to the cupboard and sink, the 'kitchen' area, barking out commands*) Open the cupboard door! Take out that can of soup! Chicken noodle soup, fine! Open it up!

SHELLEY: How do I open it. . . .

PETER: Where is the can-opener? You need a can-opener.

SHELLEY: (*turning the can around helplessly in her hands*) There is no place to get a hole started, no place that is indented . . . my fingernails are breaking. . . .

PETER: No, you need a can-opener. What did you do with the can-opener?

SHELLEY: (*looking around feverishly*) The can-opener....

PETER: It must be here someplace. Where did you put it? How could you lose it? Your brain must be like a sieve! (*a pause*) I wonder what you think about when I'm not with you. Do you think at all? Do you think of opening yourself up with the can-opener and escaping me?

SHELLEY: No, I love you....

PETER: What?

SHELLEY: I love you, only you....

PETER: (*discovering the can-opener on the floor; kicking it over to her*) Here it is! The mysterious goddam can-opener!

(SHELLEY *picks it up. Awkwardly, dreamily, she mimes opening the can, and pours its contents into a pan. She turns on the hot plate, etc., moving sluggishly.*)

PETER: What's that, the faucet dripping? It's more than a drip, it's a constant trickle. No wonder you can't wake up, you're hypnotized by that sound. Good. Water—waves—the ocean. It reminds us of our first home, the ocean. We can sleep better, awash in that sound. It's good for us. It calms our nerves. (*shouting*) Don't stand there staring at me! Get to work! He'll be home in a few minutes, you've got to look good to him—why are you trying to embarrass me?

SHELLEY: (*pressing her hands against her chest, as if out of breath, exhausted*) What is his name again...? Gordon?

PETER: No.

SHELLEY: Is it Arthur?

PETER: Arthur belongs to the past. An extreme personality, but charming—not that I blame him for what he did to you. He had every right. I don't defend him because I am a man, defending another man; I defend him because his taste turned out to be better than I had suspected. No, Arthur is gone.

SHELLEY: Then it's...Brockwood? Brockway? What was his name again...?

PETER: Brockway disappeared, the bastard. Forget about him and fix yourself up for your new husband Martin. Martin Raven. Now do you remember?

SHELLEY: (*slowly*) I remember him. I think I remember him. You took me to your place, and to the bathroom there...you ran hot water in the sink...you washed my hair.... You were so loving, your hands, the smell of the shampoo...did you love me then?

(PETER *is looking through a small notebook he has taken out of his pocket; he pays no attention to* SHELLEY.)

SHELLEY: Yes, you loved me. My knees kept buckling and you held me steady with your own knees, your legs, your thighs...you loved me...you washed my hair, you shampooed it with green shampoo that burst into lovely white bubbles, sliding through your fingers, like blossoms...you were whistling under your breath.... The soap ran into my eye and I screamed because it stung so. You had to hold me still. I was crazy that day, so strung-out...I don't blame you.... You had to press my face down in the water to make me stop screaming.... And then you rinsed my hair out and dried it in a big white towel. You, yourself, drying my hair! Peter himself! With so much work and so many people hanging on you, needing you...you took the time to wash my hair and then you dried it for me and then you put my dress on me and zipped it up the back, and helped me walk...and we met this man, this new man... what is his name again...?

PETER: You aren't as stupid as you pretend! Wake up!

SHELLEY: I can almost remember him.... We were sitting in a parked car? Was that it?

PETER: (*shaking her*) Martin Raven is his name!

SHELLEY: Martin Raven. Martin. Yes. Martin Raven. Martin Raven. Martin Raven.

PETER: You could do a little more with yourself. Perfume behind the ears, a little more bounce to your walk, fluff out your hair— You aren't really old yet, you know. You have years left. Here, let me straighten your eyebrows a little. (*wets his finger, 'fixes' her up, etc.*) You look as if you've been sleeping on your face for three days! Let's see. Your skin is still good. A few pimples on the forehead, but we can fix that—cover it up with your bangs. Like this.

Cute. How is your breath? Eh, it isn't very fresh! It smells dried, parched, stale, it smells like this room—and what's this, scum on your teeth? A film of scum on your teeth? (*He rubs at her teeth with his forefinger.*) Who is going to want to kiss you, when your breath is stale and there's scum on your teeth? You will lose your popularity if you're not careful!

(SHELLEY *embraces him;* PETER *is annoyed but tries not to show it.*)

PETER: What's wrong? Are you sniffling? Are you catching a cold?

SHELLEY: I'm sorry.

PETER: You're not wiping your nose on my shirt, are you? Are you sick?

SHELLEY: My mind is not right. I can't wake up. I can't see the corners of the room.

PETER: Are you catching a cold, that's what I asked.

SHELLEY: I don't know.

PETER: A little girl started out like this—sniffling—then her throat got sore. I looked in her mouth and it was all white with red spots. She started coughing, she couldn't breathe, she kept spitting up mucous. That wasn't so cute, all that mucous! Her cuteness came to an end. I said goodbye and started her walking down the sidewalk to where the patrol car is usually parked, and that was the end of that. I don't want that to happen to you. First the sniffling— then the sore throat—then the pneumonia or whatever it was— then they disappear. I don't want that to happen to you.

SHELLEY: No—please—

PETER: Make yourself look pretty. Hurry up. It never used to take you this long. Smile. Come on, smile.

SHELLEY: I need some of those white things—

PETER: First smile.

SHELLEY: (*confused*) Smile. How do I smile? How does it go again...?

PETER: (*putting his hands around her head and shaking it*) Is your brain turning to mucous? Are you dissolving? Wake up!

SHELLEY: Tell me what to do—

PETER: Smile! Like this! (*With his fingers he forces her mouth into a smile, which she holds, frozen.*) That's better.

SHELLEY: Tell me what else to do. I can't remember. Should I move my hands around when I talk? Should I toss my hair? Where is the ceiling? Is it a low ceiling or a high ceiling? I'm sort of afraid of bumping my head.... How far down are my feet from my head? I'm afraid I might knock my chin against my knees. Tell me what to do.

PETER: Go to the stove. See how supper is progressing. Fast! (*clapping his hands*) You are in the center of the city and in the center of America. Between your legs is the center of the world. You possess everything. You're as old as Buddha. You're immortal because you're a female. You mustn't let Peter V. down. You mustn't drag him down with you.

SHELLEY: (*puppet-like*) If I reach out with my hand I can touch things. I see this hand; I see it reaching out. It's my own hand. I'm sure of that. Here is something that is not my hand.... (*picking up a knife, turning it in the air*) It wasn't in my hand a second ago. It's something different from myself.... It's dazzling. The light hurts my eyes. It has something to do with the parts of my brain that are always going on and off, winking on and off, like lights. They're lighting up now. It's like sparks, all that activity in my head! (*turning, laughing;* PETER *is looking through his notebook again*) It's like electricity, or bubbles in soda pop.... Peter explained to me that he loved me. He said it was fate. He did love me. He told me that I did not exist. He told me not to worry. He told me he would take care of me. He told me I was light as smoke, lovely in his arms, he entered me and the whole world entered me with him, flowing along my veins, making my veins bulge so that I thought they would burst.... And is that true, Peter, that I don't exist?

PETER: (*absent-mindedly*) Absolutely. You do not exist.

SHELLEY: That I have no name?

PETER: I designate the spot you occupy by the word "Shelley." After all, we found that name in your billfold. It seemed a convenient word. You identified yourself in bright blue ink as "Shelley," on the card called "Identification," and on your driver's license there was another name, "Michele." So I could call you one name or the other. I could call you "S" or "M." Also "Shell." Or "Michael," or "Mitch" or "Mitya." Or "X." You would be obliged to answer. Or any one of a cascade of names here, if one opened up for your use. Some of these names are adorable! (*flips through notebook; addresses audience*) Listen to this—lovely names, lovely American sounds—Debby, Rose Ann, Ruthie, Dora Lee, Suzy, Bitsy, Dolly, Blondie, Annie, Kitsie, Kitty—

(*As he speaks* SHELLEY *approaches him with the knife raised, as if hypnotized.*)

SHELLEY: You love them and not me....

PETER: Franny, Barbie, Sylvie, Laurie, Trixie, Shelley, Nancy, Kathy....

SHELLEY: (*screaming*) You love them and not me!

(SHELLEY *runs at him with the knife.* PETER *backs up, alarmed.*)

PETER: Of course I love them! I love all of them and I love you. They are your sisters. You should love them yourself!

SHELLEY: You love them and not me!

PETER: You are only names in my book, why are you upset? You know what your place is among them! You are lovely little girls, you are lovely little names. None of you exist. You are only names in my book, don't worry, you are all loved equally, I will take care of you, you would all have died years ago except for lovers like me—

SHELLEY: (*shaking her head*) You love them and not me!

PETER: I love them and I love you. I love all of you. It's all the same girl. What would you do without me? I tunnel inside you, I put you to sleep, I liberate you, I take you gently apart in handfuls, I put you back together again, I take you apart, I put you back together, I take you apart, I put you back together—

SHELLEY: I want to be the only one you love! Only me!

PETER: But there isn't any you. What do you mean?

SHELLEY: (*about to rush at him*) I can see you. I know you. I can see my hand. I can see this knife. I am going to kill you, *I* am going to kill you.... *I am going* to kill you.... I know that I am going to do something after all these weeks, it's myself that will do it, *I* am going to do it....

PETER: (*with his arms outspread, smiling*) Yes, but why?

SHELLEY: Why...?

PETER: Why are you going to do it?

SHELLEY: (*confused*) Why...? I don't know....

PETER: It isn't you, but an evil spirit in you. Who is it? Who is poisoning you against me?

SHELLEY: I don't understand....

PETER: Is it another man? Your father, maybe? You mentioned your father... you thought he was following you? Is he following you? Is his spirit inside you right now?

SHELLEY: I don't know...I can't remember.... Why am I standing here, what am I going to do?

PETER: That dripping faucet is what you should listen to! Listen to it — learn from it — concentrate upon it — make it your meditation! Do you understand? Your meditation — your rosary. The cords in your neck, dear girl, are standing out; you make yourself ugly; I see tiny white lines beginning in your face — at the corners of your eyes, bracketing your mouth. Remember that silly little girl from — where was it — Arkansas — and what happened to her — screaming at one of her husbands — coming at poor Peter with a paring knife that wouldn't have pared a *carrot* —

SHELLEY: Arkansas? It was — West Virginia — We talked — we whispered together — she told me — (*pausing*) She told me lies —

PETER: Love me. Relax. Forget your father. He won't find you. He's evil: forget him. If he finds you he'll lose you again: it has happened before. Do you understand? Do you know what Peter is saying? He's evil — he's — *inconsequential*. Nothing is transmitted with the genes. Why are you looking at me so strangely, Shelley? *I'm* not your father! You *love* me! It's proper that there should be love between us because I am *not* your father. Why should you want to kill me, dear, when you love me? ...When you love me?

SHELLEY: (*vaguely*) I was going to...going to do something....

PETER: You know you love me.

SHELLEY: I love you, yes....

PETER: Of course. Now finish supper.

SHELLEY: (*turning, baffled*) It must be my father. You're right. His spirit is inside me, poisoning me. I know he's going to find me. He won't give up until he finds me. (*She lets the knife fall to the floor.*) The other time I left home he found me in three days. He notified the police everywhere in the state. Everyone knew about me. I couldn't get away. *Runaway,* they called me, they wrote that down. But they were very nice to me. That was years ago, I was only a child then . . . my father came and took me in his arms and we wept together. . . . Last year I left home again but I got sick. My insides ached. I got the flu from something I ate in a restaurant in the bus station . . . I was very sick . . . so I went to the police myself, I turned myself in. My father was only a few hours behind me. He drove down and picked me up. This time I've been away for weeks, I can hardly remember my home, it seems that I've been away for years and that I'm a different person, that everything has changed . . . when I think back (*in an attitude of painful thought*) I can't really remember that home . . . it's like a glacier has come down over it . . . everything is frozen back there, the people frozen, and there is a girl who used to be myself who is frozen there, a child. . . . What if my father finds me here?

PETER: Don't worry, he won't find you.

SHELLEY: He'll find me, he'll make me go back home with him. . . .

PETER: He can't make you do anything. I'll protect you.

SHELLEY: I don't want to be that girl again, I don't want to be Shelley. He'll try to take me in his arms and he'll cry over me, he'll make me cry again . . . I want to forget him, I want to forget Shelley. . . . I cut off her hair to spite her and I went without eating to spite her, to make her thin, very thin, to make her dizzy from not eating, to kill her!

PETER: You did right. You got her weight down to ninety-five pounds; you're very chic now, like a model! I prefer girls as thin as possible, so thin I can fit their delicate little wrists between my teeth, I prefer skin transparent like yours, it's the latest style! And your hair is long enough like that. I'll cut it a little with a razor in a few days. There are some men who like girls that are boys, and some men who like boys that are really girls; the market must be accommodated. How else can we make contact with other people except by accommodating them . . . ? We need our bodies for that. We need our bodies for communion with others. The age craves communion! We can't deny our deepest impulses! Why did you want to be Shelley, then, why did you want to kill me? Did you want to return to your old self, to that particular body and that particular name, did you want to forget me, did you want to belong again to your father and a woman said to be your mother, why did you want all that again when it never pleased you...did it? You hated it!

SHELLEY: (*dully*) Yes, I hated it....

PETER: You hated your father and your mother. Your father especially.

SHELLEY: (*more emphatically*) Yes, I hated them! Him especially... because he loved me more than she did.... He kept after me with his love, he wanted to own me, he wants to take me back with him.... My father is a doctor. He wants to cure everyone. He wants to clean them up, he wants to fix things, he wants to put bandages on everything, sterilize everything, he wanted me always to wash my hands after I went to the bathroom, he was always spying on me! He wouldn't let me alone! He loved me too much! He wouldn't let me be like the water coming out of that faucet, trickling away, emptying itself out....

PETER: (*to the audience*) I had no father, myself. I named myself. I gave birth to myself. I read a certain novel, I came across the character of Peter Verkhovansky, he leapt back into the vacancy that was myself, and I gave birth to myself at the age of twenty-five! I introduced myself to everyone as Peter V., because they would not understand that I am really Peter Verkhovansky of Dostoyevsky's great novel *The Possessed*. Peter came to America; he lost his political fervor; he became an American, a capitalist. He became me. I became him. But no one can understand that, not even this sympathetic young lady here, not even you, really there is no one who can appreciate me, and so I don't explain myself. I had no father. I was born at the age of twenty-five. Therefore I have no Oedipal complex, I have no superego, in fact I have no unconscious at all. I am pure consciousness. I am pure ego.

SHELLEY: My father is coming to get me—I'm afraid—

PETER: He can't bring the police. They need a warrant. You're untouchable, you have every right to live here, in this room, for the rest of your life. Remember that!

SHELLEY: If he comes here and calls me by name—

PETER: I'll protect you.

SHELLEY: Listen! I hear someone coming.

PETER: There's nothing.

(*They listen; there is no sound.*)

SHELLEY: (*panicked*) Yes, he's coming! I can hear his footsteps! He's on the stairs...he must have found out about this room...he must have had a detective looking for me.... There's nowhere I can go that he can't find me....

PETER: I don't hear anyone....

SHELLEY: Listen! He's on the stairs!

PETER: Don't be frightened, what's wrong with you? I said I'd protect you. It might be Martin Raven coming home....

SHELLEY: Footsteps....

PETER: (*watching the door*) Remember that you belong to me. Relax. You belong here. With me. None of this is your fault. You belong to me and to no one else, not even yourself. You're in love. You are sometimes high as the ceiling, bouncing around against the ceiling, you are sometimes flat against the floor, your nostrils pressed to a crack in the floor, you are mine, you are not to blame, you're in love....

(*There is a knock at the door.* PETER *and* SHELLEY *do not respond. The door is opened and Shelley's* FATHER *appears. He is a well-dressed, distraught man in his forties; he carries a small suitcase. He enters and he and* SHELLEY *stare at each other.*)

PETER: (*amiably*) How do you do? Have we met? Are you looking for someone? Why have you entered our apartment without knocking? Are you a stranger here? This is my building, didn't you see the sign downstairs—*condemned by order of the fire department?* (*He laughs.*) Not looking for a place to hide out, are you? What is your business with Mrs. Raven and myself?

FATHER: ...Mrs. Raven...?

(SHELLEY *shakes her head, no, as if answering her father against her will.*)

FATHER: (*quietly*) What's happened to you?

(SHELLEY *stares at him and does not reply.* FATHER *is stunned, baffled. He keeps passing his fingers through his hair.*)

PETER: If you have any questions, address them to me. Why don't you introduce yourself? My name is Peter V., a friend of the young lady's, a businessman, a kind of Ariel—

FATHER: (*to* SHELLEY) My God, you've lost weight.... What's happened to you? Are you sick? Your hair has been cut so short....

PETER: (*trying to shake hands with him*) I said my name is Peter V., I am a businessman and a friend of the young lady's. You'd better shake hands with me. I'll call the police and have you thrown out. I don't think you're a gentleman, to walk in here like this.... I have friends among the police. I have friends everywhere. You'd better explain yourself.

FATHER: You know who I am.

PETER: What do you want with us?

FATHER: I want to take her back with me....

(SHELLEY *turns away; she laughs contemptuously.* PETER *joins in her laughter and manages to force* FATHER *to shake hands with him.*)

PETER: But what is your claim? Who are you?

FATHER: You know who I am, I'm Shelley's father....

PETER: The girl in this room with us is not necessarily Shelley. She is not necessarily your daughter. Are you making a claim?

FATHER: What did you do to her? She's sick, isn't she?

PETER: I saved her life.

FATHER: Can she—can she hear us? Can she understand what we're saying?

PETER: She can hear us if I give her permission.

FATHER: Shelley....

PETER: Shelley, come here! Look at her! She's playful as a kitten, as a puppy! There's something so innocent about her.... She's a piece of matter the spirit has left, it's drained out and left her very innocent. Her soul drained out through the cracks of her darling little body, through its various delicate clefts and holes!—isn't that right, Shelley? Come here and stand by me. You can listen to us if you want to. Isn't she beautiful? She pretends to be sicker than she is. They all do. They want to be pitied and cuddled and then they change their minds, they get afraid, they run away, and then they change their minds again and weep because they have no one to hold them, they can't determine the limitations of their bodies unless someone is always with them, embracing them. Oh, they change their minds twenty times a day! They slip in and out of their minds like clothing! All of them want to die in a man's embrace, the life squeezed out of them, a big bear hug, a cosmic bear hug? Look at her. Between her legs the universe opens up— that darkness, that lovely dark machinery!—but she doesn't know it, she's too far gone.

FATHER: What's wrong with her...?

PETER: We must talk man to man. Of course you're not her father. You've looked me up to make a deal with me; you want the girl for yourself. Right?

FATHER: Shelley, are you ready to come home with me?

(SHELLEY *laughs wildly, waving him away. She 'poses,' arching her back, moving coquettishly.* PETER *rubs his hands.*)

PETER: If I seriously thought you were this girl's father, barging in here to ruin her life, to take her back to that prison, I would call the police and have them beat you up. After all, this building is mine! I bought it for $10,000 on a land contract last May and only three years ago it was worth $110,000—think of that! Everything in this city is falling—the tax base, the sidewalks, the streets, everything! It's a time when people like myself have only to stoop to pick up prizes; all we have to do is bend over. Our talent thrives in such troubled times! Ah, we are the truest Americans, the truest talents! —Are you listening to me? I don't believe you're this girl's father. Tell us who you are.

(SHELLEY *stands beside* PETER, *her head against his shoulder; he 'cuddles' her.*)

FATHER: (*rubbing his eyes, very confused*) What are you talking about...? I can't understand you....

PETER: You understand me well enough!

FATHER: I haven't slept for two days.... I've been calling home to see if Shelley is back yet, but every time I call it's the same, nothing ever changes.... Your mother says you died and you should be forgotten. But I can't forget.

PETER: (*cheerfully*) You're telling us lies! You're making all this up!

FATHER: Once I saw a girl on the street, in Toledo, and I ran after her thinking it was you....

PETER: What's in that suitcase?

FATHER: A projector—

PETER: What?

FATHER: A projector—for slides and films—

PETER: Home movies?

FATHER: Let me explain. Please. You are always interrupting me—

PETER: But we're listening, we're fascinated!

FATHER: I put together some things to show her—if I found her—I wanted to explain myself to her—

PETER: Explain what?

FATHER: I want to be logical and objective. I don't want to force her to do anything.

PETER: What have you got, home movies?

FATHER: Some slides made from snapshots. A few things. I put it together before I left home...a few things to show her.... There is something I must prove to her.

SHELLEY: (*violently*) *He* saved my life, not you! Peter saved my life!

FATHER: Shelley....

SHELLEY: He made me into the dark side of the world. Most of the world is water. I bet you didn't know that! You can sink in it forever, that dark water, it's always moving, pulsating, ebbing, flowing, streaming, draining away, flowing back, flooding, rising, crashing.... Try to stop it! You can't! He made me into that water, he made me the dark side of the world, he saved my life by kissing me, it was a kiss that lasted for hours, for days.... He breathed into my mouth, he breathed himself into me.

FATHER: You're not well. You're—

SHELLEY: I can't hear you. I'm not even listening. I'm not your daughter or anyone's daughter. I don't remember anything. I am not convinced that anything ever happened to me. I don't remember. If Peter exists then I exist, but only when he's in the same room with me. He's gone most of the time. I wait for him and when he returns I come alive again. There is nothing that anyone else can say to me. (*a sudden gesture of anger, embarrassment*) Oh, that stupid thing! That projector of yours! You were always embarrassing us, taking pictures all the time—birthdays, Christmas, Easter Sunday, graduation!—how I hated that, being herded around and made to smile, to look pretty, you with your camera trying to put us all on film!

FATHER: You wanted me to take pictures of you—

SHELLEY: I did not!

FATHER: And you loved to watch the movies we made—the whole family loved them!

SHELLEY: I was lying to you.

FATHER: What do you mean? You weren't lying.... Now your voice is so strange.... It's as if someone else were speaking for you.

(SHELLEY *waves him away.*)

FATHER: Who is this man, Shelley? What did he do to you?

PETER: (*courteously*) I have already introduced myself....

SHELLEY: (*to* FATHER) To you I lied, I was a lie myself—my body was rotten with lies. To him I tell the truth. I tell Peter everything.

FATHER: Who is he?

SHELLEY: A man who saved my life!

PETER: (*to* FATHER) Why don't you open up your suitcase? I'm anxious to see what you have. Is it an expensive outfit? I'm thinking of getting a movie camera myself, but I'm careful about buying things, I go slowly, I consider a purchase like that quite an investment. I think I'd wait for sales in January.

SHELLEY: (*her hands to her face*) I don't want to look at anything he has. Nothing of his. Nothing he has to show me.

FATHER: (*opening the suitcase, moving slowly and apologetically*) Shelley, please... I put together a few things to show you.... You don't have to do anything. I won't force you to do anything.

SHELLEY: I won't look!

PETER: (*examining the projector*) This looks like a good piece of equipment. Where did you get it?

SHELLEY: Make him leave! There's nothing of my life I want to look at—it's finished—

PETER: Photographs show us the flatness of our bodies. They're really two-dimensional, our bodies. They would be one-dimensional if they could be, but unfortunately one-dimensional things are invisible. The soul is one-dimensional, if it exists. That's why I like photographs and the apparatus that makes photographs possible. I'm grateful to you for coming here this afternoon!

FATHER: (*abruptly*) Get away from there?

PETER: (*cringing, fawning, mocking*) Are you afraid I'll contaminate your machine?

FATHER: I don't want you touching it.

PETER: My fingers are absolutely clean. I'm sterile inside and out. You're a doctor and you think people must be crawling with germs, and only you can save them. But I'm absolutely clean.

FATHER: (*confused*) I'm sorry... for losing my temper.... I haven't slept for a while.... And what is that, that noise? I keep hearing a noise....

PETER: Just a facuet. Does it make you nervous?

FATHER: A faucet...?

(SHELLEY *runs to the sink. She tries to stop the water by sticking her finger up the faucet.*)

SHELLEY: (*laughing*) Nothing can stop this! We need a plumber up here. It's been dripping for weeks, it's made the sink rusty, there's a rust-colored ring in the sink.... In a few more weeks it will wear the sink away and leak out onto the floor.

FATHER: I'm a little nervous, my hands are shaky....

PETER: It's too bad you haven't slept. Would you like to sleep here, on our mattress? We'd be very quiet—we'd tip-toe around and speak only in whispers.

FATHER: No... no.... I want to...I want to show Shelley these things, and then I'll leave if she wants me to....

(FATHER *sets up the apparatus, moving clumsily.*)

PETER: (*goes briskly to the right to turn off the lights, so that the stage is dim but not dark; he returns to center stage, rubbing his hands*) I'll turn off the lights! Excellent! So you want to interfere with our souls, eh? You want to display yourself to us? You know, in antiquity the gods did not interfere with souls; they were content to maim bodies. You might be walking out in ordinary sunlight and a hand would grab your hair and lift you up into the sky—no surprise! You had to expect such things. Or, because two gods loved you, you might be gored to death by an animal with fabulous tusks, perhaps an animal invented right at that moment.... But you fathers want to be newer gods; you want to interfere with our souls, your children's souls. But you won't succeed. We no longer have any souls.

FATHER: (*as the first slide flashes on the wall—a snapshot of a man and a woman, black and white*) Shelley, this is my mother and father. The year is 1922.

SHELLEY: (*angrily*) What do I care about your mother and father?

FATHER: Your grandparents....

SHELLEY: I don't have any grandparents! Anyway I've seen that picture before. I don't know those people, I have nothing to do with them! They're dead!

PETER: They're strangely ugly people, aren't they?

SHELLEY: They're dead!

FATHER: My father was about twenty-five when this was taken. He was a very energetic man, a wonderful man...he liked to hunt...he bought a gas station and worked very hard, but he lost money... everything went wrong.... He lost everything in the thirties. He lost his will to live.

SHELLEY: (*hysterically*) I don't want to hear this! It's all dead, all finished! It's like breathing into me, opening me up the way Peter did. They want to pump love into you. Everyone wants to pump love into everyone else.

PETER: It's inconclusive, however. Everyone—nearly everyone—has grandparents.

FATHER: (*as another slide comes on*) My family. My parents, and my two sisters and my brother....

PETER: And yourself. I would recognize you anywhere.

FATHER: This was taken in 1935.

PETER: You were a skinny kid. Look at those eyes! Christ, you're staring at us—everything is in those eyes! (*walks up to the wall, peering at the picture*)

FATHER: (*as another slide appears*) Your mother and I....

SHELLEY: I don't want to see this!

FATHER: ...before we were married. I was twenty-four then. Wasn't your mother pretty? She was such a pretty woman.

PETER: Is she dead now?

FATHER: Of course not. She's waiting for us back home.

PETER: I thought all those people were dead.

FATHER: They're living, they're not dead.... (*as another slide appears*) And this—this is Shelley—only a few weeks old—

(*There is silence.*)

FATHER: (*to* SHELLEY) What are you thinking?

(SHELLEY *turns away.*)

FATHER: Are you—are you well enough to understand what I'm showing you?

PETER: She's afraid of crowds. You brought a crowd into the room.

FATHER: I don't understand you.

PETER: She came running out of a crowd and into my arms, this girl you claim as your daughter. It's the same protoplasm as the infant up on the wall, I suppose, but you can't prove it. Really, you can't prove anything. The crowd opened up and a girl ran toward me, I could see she was terrified, she needed love, she needed me to mythologize her. So I took her in my arms. I saved her from the crowd. You're bringing the crowd back, you're confusing her.

FATHER: Shelley? Come here.

(*When she does not immediately respond,* PETER *snaps his fingers.* SHELLEY *approaches him as if against her will. Her hands are pressed against her face.*)

SHELLEY: I can't see anything.

FATHER: More pictures of Shelley... eight months old... a year old... eighteen months... two years... three years... this was taken on Christmas Day 1957....

SHELLEY: Stop it!

FATHER: Your sister Jeanne....

SHELLEY: I don't have any sister!

FATHER: Easter Sunday—

PETER: The sister is quite pretty!

FATHER: Shelley in high school, fourteen years old....

SHELLEY: It isn't me! Go to hell!

FATHER: Another picture of Shelley. Her mother took it; that's me in the background. Do you recognize this, Shelley? Cape Cod. Do you recognize that bathing suit, Shelley? That tiger kitten that belonged to the neighbors' children....

SHELLEY: My head is being blown up like a balloon. You're killing me. If my head gets much bigger I'll float up against the ceiling... you'll have to pull me down by grabbing hold of my ankles....

FATHER: This was taken the same day. Look at her beautiful long hair!

PETER: Did you love her?

FATHER: Why—why do you speak in the past tense?

PETER: Do you love her?

FATHER: Yes, I love her. I only followed her here to talk with her, quietly. To show her these things. I don't want to force her into anything, I want to prove something to her, I won't make demands upon her...I want to prove something to her....

SHELLEY: He wants to prove that I exist!

PETER: (*motioning her away*) Calm down, please. There's an odor released from you when you're excited. It isn't very cute. Men don't smell like that.

SHELLEY: I'm not a man but I'm not a girl either. I'm not male and I'm not female. Look at that ugly body in the picture! That body! Breasts and hips and legs and long hair and that smile, that stupid smile! I could hack that girl into pieces with a knife! I could tear her into pieces with my teeth!

FATHER: This one was taken in the fall...the light was a little dim....

PETER: The three women in your family, eh? Your wife and your two daughters.... Why did you take all these pictures?

FATHER: Because....

PETER: Why do Americans take so many pictures?

FATHER: Because...because....

SHELLEY: They want to prove that they exist!

PETER: Don't stand so near me. You smell like that mattress, you smell like blood....

SHELLEY: I don't smell of blood!

PETER: Your underwear was stained when I first met you.

FATHER: (*as if not hearing*) And this is your mother on her birthday last year. Remember those flowers? Your mother was saying, just as I took this picture, "It won't turn out, it's too dark in here...."

SHELLEY: He's bringing everyone in this room!

FATHER: Another of Shelley. Look at that smile! She knows she's much prettier than her sister...she seems to offer her face up to the camera like a flower, a lovely flower....

SHELLEY: They are all coming in this room, all of them....

(SHELLEY *rushes at* FATHER *and tries to knock the projector over.* FATHER *takes hold of her and they struggle.*)

SHELLEY: He's touching me! I can feel him touching me!

(*In the struggle the apparatus is knocked over.* PETER *tries to pull* SHELLEY *away.*)

SHELLEY: It doesn't prove anything—

FATHER: Shelley, what's wrong with you? Stop—

SHELLEY: (*screaming*) There's nothing there! Pictures! I didn't see them —they're not real— You failed! You failed to convince me!

(PETER *turns the lights on, hurrying. Then he crosses to* SHELLEY *and tries to calm her.*)

PETER: You're hysterical. Be quiet.

FATHER: I'm taking you home with me—

SHELLEY: (*screaming*) You failed! Failed!

PETER: (*righting the projector, gathering the slides together*) It was an interesting interlude, but now we must return to real life. All this emotion is embarrassing. The girl's husband will be home at any minute. She has certain duties she must perform for him. Everything in the past is buried, nobody cares about the past, shovelfuls of time have buried it. Leave us. Go away.

FATHER: No, she's coming back with me—

PETER: What do you want with a girl like that? She's too far gone. She's not much good, believe me.

FATHER: (*shoving* PETER) I'll kill you—

(PETER *jumps to his feet and pushes* FATHER *away.*)

PETER: (*scornfully*) An old god! Old mythology! Go to hell!

FATHER: I'll call the police—

PETER: I'll have the police kick your teeth out, you old bastard!

FATHER: I—I'll—

SHELLEY: (*her hands to her face*) Make him leave!

PETER: Now you must leave, really. Everything is over. The lights are on and it's embarrassing now.

FATHER: But I had more pictures yet.... And I didn't explain the ones I showed, I had more to say, much more...everything went so quickly, it was so confused.... I had more to say. I should have written it down....

SHELLEY: Make him leave!

PETER: This is my building and you must leave. I don't like to speak harshly to a man your age, but....

(*The door opens suddenly and* MARTIN RAVEN *enters. He is a heavy-set man of ordinary appearance, rather pale. He is startled at seeing the father.*)

PETER: (*cheerfully*) Hello, Martin!

MARTIN: What's all this?

PETER: He's just leaving.

MARTIN: He looks like trouble. He looks like a detective....

PETER: No, that isn't it. He's a friend of the girl's but he's leaving.

FATHER: Who is this?

PETER: Her young husband has just come home; their domestic life must begin; there is no room for you. Private life is sacred.

FATHER: Shelley —

SHELLEY: Don't make me look at you!

(FATHER *hesitates, then puts his things together slowly and prepares to leave.* SHELLEY *stands with her back to him, her hands pressed against her face.*)

PETER: (*to* FATHER) You don't exist to her. You're just a beak and claw fluttering around her head; she's always dreaming about that kind of thing; she dreams of crowds. Up here, we take care of her. We love her.

FATHER: But I can't leave her here....

MARTIN: Who the hell is this guy?

PETER: (*briskly*) Sit down and relax! You've had a hard day at the Post Office, right? You want some supper, right? You want some loving, right? This gentleman is on his way out.

FATHER: But if I leave.... (*appealing to her*) If I leave, Shelley, I won't return....

MARTIN: (*frightened and insolent*) Look, you, get the hell out of here! I don't like the looks of things!

FATHER: Shelley...?

SHELLEY: (*sinking to the floor; weakly yet stubbornly*) I don't hear anything! Anyone's voice! There is no Shelley—you can't claim me— I don't *hear* you—go away, leave me—go away—

FATHER: Shelley...?

(*Silence.* FATHER *picks up the suitcases and leaves.*)

PETER: (*after applauding her performance, mockingly yet robustly*) Very good! Very...very good. Now, my girl, let's set you going again.... (*He heaves her to her feet. She begins to fall again; roughly, he holds her up; steadies her.*) Come on, come on. We've been extremely patient.... (*Her knees threaten to buckle again; but finally he manages to steady her. He releases her, experimentally.*) All right? Fine? He's gone and he won't return and you're safe: right?

(SHELLEY *mutely acquiesces.*)

PETER: (*playfully*) All right? Yes? Forever and ever and ever? 'Till death—? *Right?* (*a pause*) 'Till death.

(*A long pause. Then an abrupt change in the mood and pacing of the play: a sort of bawdy fast-moving humor.*)

MARTIN: What the hell was that all about? I thought nobody knew about her up here. What if the cops come? Who's been talking?

PETER: Relax, take off your shoes. Take off your coat. Did you smell supper as you came up the stairs?

MARTIN: The hell with supper. I'm not eating here.

(MARTIN *crosses to* SHELLEY *and takes hold of her by the back of the neck and shakes her.*)

MARTIN: You! I don't trust you—you're sweating like a pig! You smell like a pig!

(SHELLEY *is passive in his hands; she submits to being shaken, mauled.*)

PETER: I guarantee you that she has not been unfaithful. I was here all along.

MARTIN: (*flat, rapid voice*) I can't stay all night this time. My mother is suspicious. She asks about me—worries about me—I'm only thirty-two—my health isn't good. I'm susceptible to colds, sore throats.... What if I catch a disease from this little maniac, how could I tell my mother? I'd be so ashamed!

PETER: (*at the sink; washing his face*) She's absolutely clean, I swear it. You worried excessively about the one from Arkansas, don't you remember, and it came to nothing.

MARTIN: (*suspiciously*) But she wasn't—she wasn't very strong. She didn't last.

PETER: (*chuckling*) You were a little rough with her.

MARTIN: The one Freddy had, from West Virginia—

PETER: Never mind about Freddy: that doesn't concern you.

MARTIN: She lasted a lot longer. She put up a real *fight.* (*turning to* SHELLEY) Who are you gaping at? Whose face are you memorizing? What are you, anyway? Beneath these things? A little boy, a skinny little girl? —Don't you resist *me!*

(MARTIN *and* SHELLEY *struggle together.* SHELLEY *cries out;* MARTIN *claps his hand over her mouth; throws her down. The lights fade on them, and concentrate upon* PETER, *now shaving at the sink.*)

PETER: There are risks, and there are rewards. One has doubts—naturally! But one continues. I don't at all mind the competition—it's healthy, it's American—it's in our great tradition—I thrive on it, in fact—I find it exhilarating. I am a vigorous young man standing at a sink in a condemned building—but it's *my* building—and I have controlled the scenario. I take pride in my existence—pride enough to shave. *My* face is very real, and has never been photographed. You can't catch and make permanent my—essence. Not mine. My face is real, I am said to be quite handsome, that's neither here nor there, I control the definitions, I control the terms of commerce, I navigate the seven seas, I do a great deal of smiling.

...Now *that* worries me, upon occasion. For what if all this smiling wears my face out? *My* face? The way water wears out porcelain? (*a pause*) Will we all wear out, then? *Must* we? Like Shelley...last year's Shelley...whatever her name.... Must our existences be so cruelly questioned? (*He pauses, contemplating the audience. Sincere, forthright, man-to-man.*) These are all legitimate, indeed profound issues, which we may take up at another time, in more congenial surroundings. Unfortunately I'm rather rushed: and I find this setting rather depressing, as I'm sure you do. Another time—? I'm *really* in rather a hurry.

(*Lights fade to blackout.*)

MIRACLE PLAY

for
Daniel Freudenberger

Miracle Play was first presented by the New Phoenix Repertory Company at the Playhouse II Theatre, 359 West 48 Street, New York City, on December 30, 1973. The cast was as follows:

Beatie Roscoe .... Marcella Lowery

Titus Skinner .... Robert Guillaume

Mason Skinner .... Ernest Thomas

Earl Roscoe .... Donny Burks

Rollie .... Ralph Wilcox

Bob Skinner .... Jaison Walker

Mrs. Skinner .... Louise Stubbs

Prosecutor .... John Benson

Kidd .... F. Murray Abraham

Conroy Roscoe .... David Connell

Directed by Daniel Freudenberger

NOTE:

The play moves in and out of three dimensions: the 'natural' in which characters speak exactly as the people they represent speak; the 'farcical' in which characters speak exactly as a strange audience might suppose them to speak, parodying both themselves and the audience; and the 'mystical' in which characters speak not as their stage selves, or as the selves they represent would speak, but as essences, as pure souls, not defined by color or age or personality of any kind.

The play should not move freely back and forth through these dimensions, however; one should sense the transition, almost a painfulness, a strain, a nearly muscular resistance. The audience should sense with what difficulty the three dimensions come together.

CHARACTERS:

Beatie Roscoe, age sixteen

Conroy Roscoe, age thirty-one

Earl Roscoe, age nineteen

Titus Skinner, age twenty-nine

Mason Skinner, age twenty-three

Mrs. Skinner, age fifty

Bob Skinner, age fourteen

Rollie, age twenty

Kidd, age thirty-five (a white man)

Prosecutor, age thirty-five (a white man)

SCENE ONE

An ordinary room, with an unmade bed, a bureau with drawers partly opened, clothing and towels lying about, a closet door standing open. It is a naturalistic scene. The door opens and BEATIE *enters, pushed through the doorway by* TITUS.

BEATIE *is wearing a yellow dress.* TITUS *is wearing a stylish suit, with a shirt of some expensive silkish material; no necktie. Throughout the play* TITUS *exhibits a certain self-consciousness, a nervous but intelligent awareness of himself, as if he is continually anticipating his own words and actions, and anticipating their effect upon others. From time to time he shows an awareness of the audience.*

BEATIE: Howcome you marched me up here? (*She is nervous, but tries to appear angry.*) What's this? This crap? This bed an' stuff, all this layin' around, you lookin' for maid-service? This ain't room service. You grabbed hold of the wrong girl.

TITUS: Just preparing a scene for a little talk. This room rings a door-bell with you...? No accidental room, huh? You know all this, huh? (*He takes her by the shoulders and forces her to look around.*)

BEATIE: (*trying to squirm away from him*) That hurts—

TITUS: (*pretending surprise*) Oh hurts? What hurts? What's that word— hurts? That an important word in your vocabulary, honey? You want to spell out that word for me?

BEATIE: I don't need to stand for this—

TITUS: Look, honey, you seen how easy it is to kidnap a cute little fox like you from right down in the street, all kinds of people hangin' around, them girl friends of yours never gave no alarm did they? You got a strong-souled boy friend, honey, to snatch you right up off the sidewalk an' march you up here, back to the scene of the crime, and a little interrogation. Now, honey, now look: I'm goin' to put a direct question to you; what did you do with that stuff?

BEATIE: (*guiltily*) What stuff?

TITUS: Five hundred dollars of it, Beatie, honey, you sneaked away with five hundred dollars of my trade, which is invested in me by sources that don't stand for no displeasure—all this is not news, right? My surprise is how dumb you are, sneakin' out like that. Night comes, dawn comes, people open their eyes an' wake up, people don't take no night-time shit from other people when the night is over— right? What did you do with it?

BEATIE: With what? With what? I don't know what the hell—

(TITUS *stands patiently, mockingly, watching her. She walks around the room, as if trying to distract him; out of the corner of her eye she sees the door to the corridor. Very subtly,* TITUS *dissuades her from trying to run for the door, by moving only an inch or so; he stands with his arms folded. He is very much in control of the scene.*)

BEATIE: I am no stranger to all of this crap, this smelly junk an' shit an' garbage you lay down in—I don't put no claim to it, either, to clean it up or make that stinkin' bed—maybe one time I would trip all over the stairs, just to put away Titus Skinner's drawers, maybe one time, yes, but I learned a certain lesson—I don't plan to be no second-time loser with you—I—I know how taken-up Titus is with his plans—(*She pauses, goes to the bed, as if to make it up. Her manner is bright, innocent.*) Can't stand to see all this mess— Long's I'm up here I might's well—

TITUS: (*ironically*) No use, Beatie. Nope. No use. You got none of the right magic to undo harm. You just a moron-brained little girl, you don't have a hint of your best advantage. Let that stuff alone.

BEATIE: (*pretending not to understand*) This is such a surprise place, judgin' from how you walk around outside—you an' them outfits

—I'm surprised you don't rent no special maid service to tend
to you—

(TITUS *tears the bedclothes away from her. He throws them down
in a heap.* BEATIE *backs away from him.*)

TITUS: You got it hid somewhere, for a joke? Blackmail joke? Or what
is it? You plannin' on usin' that stuff yourself, you graduated that
far along? Or you goin' to sell it on the street, handfuls at a time?
Where is it hid, honey? Time is runnin' short. You know I am a
busy man.

BEATIE: I don't know what—I don't know— I— You talkin' about
something I should know? Something missin' from this room?
Look Titus, (*laughing*) I am just too confused for thought—my
brain is flooded with things pictures looks like flashes of dirty bedclothes—or butterfly wings—or—

TITUS: Where is it hid? I hope to Jesus you got it hid well, Beatie,
because I am countin' on retrievin' that stuff in fifteen minutes—
today is a Friday and my Fridays are busy schedules— Where'd you
put it? You never brought it home to your momma's place, I rule
that out right away, your momma ain't goin' to lay back an' close
her eyes, *she* got to get her nose in everything! So where did you
hide it, honey?

BEATIE: Hide what?

TITUS: You want your face ripped?

BEATIE: Ripped how come?

TITUS: Oh, Jesus, you can't get through this scene, you just a damn sad
moron-brained little girl, you can't utter no lie to Titus, why,
Jesus, Titus is a boyfriend to you a hundred times over—you an'
all them girls like you—Titus asks the questions an' determines
the truth of the statement— If you can't lie better than how you
doin', honey, you ought not to trespass the law. This room is my
private place, an' the merchandise I got here, when I got it, is my
private trade, an' you got to be much wiser than Titus to violate
his territory. Now, honey, you know all this an' I believe you only
sneaked out with some bagful of stuff for a trick, because you is a
cute little girl, right?—you planned in your head a surprise for
you' nigger, how pleased he goin' to be when you tell him it was a
joke—that it? A joke? But now the joke lost its touch, honey. This

is Friday pay-day an' check-day, as you know, an' no day for a discussion. Beatie, you better tell me before I get over-excited an' out of hand —*where* you got it hid?

BEATIE: I never took nothin' from you—I never— I wasn't— I don't—

(TITUS *seizes her by the arm and shakes her.* BEATIE *breaks away.*)

BEATIE: You're crazy like a wild man—you're all out of focus—

TITUS: You stole somethin' from me an' I want it back!

BEATIE: You big damn bull—

TITUS: (*becoming angrier*) Didn't lose it, did you? Didn't trade it off, did you? Howcome you look so scared? You got instincts in your legs, girl, don't you? But I got my own instincts too. You want a workin'-over, is that so? Want some emergency-ward-work done on your face, do you? I goin' to unstitch you an' they goin' to stitch you up again—big needles an' thick black thread stitchin' you' face up again when I finish— Where you headed?

(BEATIE *runs to the window, as if to throw herself out.* TITUS *grabs her.*)

BEATIE: (*terrified*) This-here high up—out the window it's high up— How'd I get up here, third or fourth floor of some place—?

TITUS: You want to see how high up? You want to experience how high up? (*holding her in front of the window*) Beatie, I never allowed for this long a discussion, I comin' to the end of my patience.... (*pause*) You *got* that stuff, ain't you? Didn't give it away, did you? (*pause*) Beatie, honey, you didn't give it away, did you...?

BEATIE: I never...I don't know what...I don't know what you mean....

TITUS: Jesus, did you give it away...? To Conroy? Did you give it away to Conroy?

BEATIE: (*beginning to cry, but girlish, 'innocent'*) I am so mixed-up this morning...I am not myself.... What's this about Conroy? I stay clean away from Conroy....

TITUS: Was he behind it? Was he?

BEATIE: Conroy don't know my business—

TITUS: Yes, you always been close to Conroy, all of your family close together—your big-mouth momma tryin' to say she ain't ashamed of Conroy—puttin' him up, pretendin' to my momma's face he is equal to *me*— Why, Conroy on the short list! Conroy scheduled for disaster! *He* put you to stealin' that stuff, didn't he?—*he* plannin' on a vacation all his own, usin' it up day by day, five hundred dollars of a investment of *Titus's*—

BEATIE: I don't do no favors for Conroy, Conroy just a sick mess—

TITUS: You goin' to be a sickern Conroy if that stuff is gone—if he is hidin' out with it— You better be able to put your finger on where that motherfucker is hidin' or— (BEATIE *struggles with him and he shakes her violently.*) You want manhandlin'! Damn drug-out little running-sore bitch you' momma is ashamed of— Don't you try goin' sideways, you ain't disappearing into no magic. *I* handle the magic here— Where is Conroy? Did you give it to him? Where is he? You want me to track him down in person? (*becoming angrier*) Bitch! I am boxed into a situation where my connections are watchin' every move close—they got their eye on me—I don't have nobody laugh at me, up an' down the street people waitin' to laugh at me, they scared as hell face-to-face but they waitin' for me to misstep an' turn my back— You are tantalizin' me close to murder! Time I get finished with you, the doctor students goin' to have a real party-time matching up parts of you' face, down there at the morgue—you know how they do down there?—they drug the bodies out of the river or pick 'em up on the street an' lay 'em out on a table, an' perform the autopsy, white kids, studying to be doctors— Why Beatie, honey, they gonna pull stuff out of you' insides hand over hand (*He makes a comic, cruel gesture.*) an' stand around laughin' like hell—

BEATIE: (*screaming*) I never stole nothin'! Nothin' from you!

TITUS: Where is it? Where— (*suddenly calm*) I gon' punish you in style.

(*He throws her down onto the bed, and rips open the back of her dress. He picks up a metal coat hanger from the floor and raises it to strike her back.*)

BEATIE: (*screaming*) Titus— Titus—

SCENE TWO

*An unfurnished room, with a few crates, cartons, unidentified
piles of things pushed back against the wall; what appears to be a
mattress, with a single blanket loosely on it, and a few kitchenware
items: a hot-plate, plugged in; some silverware, cups, etc. on the
floor. The door opens and* MASON SKINNER *is pushed into the room,
blindfolded, by* EARL ROSCOE *and his friend* ROLLIE. ROLLIE *is
carrying a package of sugar, in a recognizable carton.*

MASON: (*speaking rapidly*) I don't know nothin' about Titus! I ain't
connected to him! First thing I heard about, about how he went
after Beatie, first thing I heard I run into the house an' told my
momma, an' I said to her *Jesus Christ! Now you see how crazy he
has got!* Earl? I know that's you there, Earl—I know it's you—
Earl?

(EARL *does not answer. He forces* MASON *to his knees, and points to
the hot-plate, a pot that is lying on the floor, and gestures that*
ROLLIE *should go out somewhere and fill the pot with water.*
ROLLIE *nods and does this.*)

MASON: (*in a voice that moves from sincere protestation through a kind
of farcical whine to terror*) Earl? Earl? Howcome you goin' after
me? I got nothin' to do with Titus! Nothin'! He don't never turn
up at the place, he sends some cash along sometimes an' bought
Momma a coat—an' a rug—but Jesus, Jesus, you know I ain't in
with him, he don't think shit of me— Earl, you know that, you
know that! Earl? Why you doin' this? Is this a kidnapping, is it to
get Titus to come around? Because—because—he ain't never goin'
to give a damn about me—

(ROLLIE *returns with a pot of water, which is set on the hot-plate.*
EARL *opens the package of sugar and shakes it near* MASON'S *face;
then he seizes* MASON'S *head and puts a pinch of sugar to his lips.*)

MASON: What's that? What?... sugar? What you goin' to do with sugar?
(*wildly*) You boilin' some water there? Is that sugar-water? What
you want to do that for, Earl, you don't plan on hurtin' me, do
you? I ain't no enemy of yours—I ain't even a real brother to Titus,
I am his half-brother— Titus always push me around, Titus is no
brother to me. Earl? Howcome you so mean, now, you turned

mean overnight? I never did no harm to you—you ask Beatie if I ain't always been nice to her—an' Beatie likes me O.K., Beatie don't know about this, does she?—Beatie? She would scream for you to stop if—

(MASON *tries to get to his feet, but they push him down to his knees again.* EARL *ties his hands behind him.*)

MASON: (*trying to be calm, then frightened, then terrified, then calm again*) Titus don't give shit for me! He's no close brother to me or none of us! He breakin' my momma's heart!— Earl, I saw it was you—*I saw it was you*—an' Rollie, is that Rollie? I known who it was! Now this got to be a joke to scare me—because there is no connection between Titus Skinner an' me or anybody else— He only goin' to laugh if you mess me up. He only goin' to *laugh.* He make fun of me all the time an' laugh at where I work, he got it in his head I am a garbage man, an' he don't let go of that, which is a lie—I am on the truck for Parks an' Recreation—an' we got rakes an' things—an' it mostly ain't garbage but just leaves an' stuff from the trees—in the park—an' run-down squirrels, shit like that, mashed things an' squashed-up, or a dog, you know, a dog if somebody run over him an' we get the call—an'—an' it ain't no garbage truck—an' Titus just laugh at me for it, he ain't no connection to me, an' it not goin' to break his heart if—if—if you—(*pause*) You ain't sincerely boilin' some water—? You ain't goin' to blame me for Beatie hurt like that, are you—? I don't know Titus's business, I don't know where he is right at this moment or any other given moment—Earl, you listen! Titus is no brother to me, no close brother—he a bastard got to cause trouble —that ain't no paid-for car of his—he not makin' nowhere like four thousand a week, like the talk has it, up an' down the street— that a lot of bullshit talk—who goin' to hand him that much money? I ask you that—? Up at the top they makin' that kind of money but Titus ain't at the top—he is a liar—what he says—he is just goin' to laugh— Earl, why ain't you talkin' to me? This is a joke to scare me? You want me to say where Titus gone, where he hidin' out—? I don't know nothin' about Titus, not one fact, not one address anywhere in this city or anywhere else—you want me to telephone him, or—?... The last time I run into him, on the street where I was walkin', an' he just drove on by in his car an' give me a nod—I think he gave me a nod—had on sunglasses like mirrors—I couldn't see where he was lookin'—I hear the talk, like you—I hear lots of wild talk—I don't know nothin' about Titus an' his life! He kicked free of all of us! He kickin' free of his old self! He ain't my close tie an' he ain't my brother—he ain't nothin' to do with me— Only goin' to laugh like hell an' say, *How come you boys messed up Mason's ugly face, already messed-up bad enough!*... You ain't goin' to dump no water on me, Earl?—how am I connected to you?—howcome you got me here, right here, kneelin' here, what am I to you an' what Titus got to do with me— or you—or anybody that is human—?

SCENE THREE

The SKINNER *living room. There are many items of furniture, including a shabby sofa.* BOB *is alone. The door opens and* MRS. SKINNER *leads* MASON *in. He is bandaged.* MASON *sits on the sofa to the left, very carefully.* MRS. SKINNER *hurries over to him and helps him lie down.*

BOB: You been out there a long time—you an' Momma—I was worried —uh—

MRS. SKINNER: (*angrily to* BOB) Turn on that television!

BOB: (*after a long pause*) Titus got to know about this... Titus got to be informed....

MASON: No.

BOB: I'm gonna get Titus onto this...gonna get him over here....

MASON: No!

BOB: You just afraid of more hurt.... But... (*gathering strength*) But I ain't afraid of it, I ain't, I'm gonna notify Titus on all of this—

MRS. SKINNER: Shut your mouth. Titus ain't in town, Titus gone.

BOB: He out of town on business but he comin' back— You know *for sure* Titus comin' back—

MASON: No—no more—they'll kill me—

MRS. SKINNER: (*to* BOB) Now you see you got him all worked up, you shootin' that mouth of yours— Mason been through a lot, honey, you got to sympathize. Mason been down at the clinic an' you know how long he was waitin'? He was waitin' a whole day long, an' he very worn-out now, an' not himself. (*to* MASON) Now you just lay still. You goin' to be fine now, you lay still an' rest. All goin' to get healed. They said come back an' get the bandage changed an' some ointment an' stuff an' we gon' do all that when the time comes, goin' to get you back to yourself again—

MASON: (*suddenly afraid*) No—they'll kill me—

MRS. SKINNER: Honey, they ain't nowhere near. Ain't goin' to get you. Honey, lay still, you shiverin' an' better lay still—(*She tries to put a blanket over him. He thrusts it away. Then, when she draws it up over him again, he acquiesces.*) In a minute you goin' be all set in place an' you can watch the show comin' on. How's that? You goin' to lay still an' rest up an' get back to yourself an' there is no hurry about nothin'—lots of shows comin' up every day—

BOB: (*to* MRS. SKINNER) Did they fix up his face?

(MRS. SKINNER *makes a gesture to silence him.*)

MASON: I hear some noise—

MRS. SKINNER: That's the television show. You don't need to look at it, honey, if your eyes waterin', you just lay there an' listen an' relax an' let them pills work on you.

MASON: There is something out there—some noise—I can hear them messin' around—

BOB: Howcome he talks so funny?

MRS. SKINNER: Your brother is tryin' to concentrate on that show an' you shut up! (*grabbing* BOB *and walking him to the other side of the room*) Look, Mason is hurt bad, he is miserable with pain an' you got to imagine it, for yourself, an' not be so damn smart. Did anybody telephone here? Did Titus call?

BOB: Telephone...? No, nobody.... You think Titus goin' to call?

MRS. SKINNER: That phone not workin' right anyway, if he wanted to call. Nobody called?

BOB: It never rung.... Maybe it don't work.

MRS. SKINNER: Beatie's momma hangin' around on the street down there, she so drunk she can't stand up. An' Beatie swingin' her ass up an' down the street, nobody never begged Beatie to run after my

Titus, an' Jesus!—she must have been exploded out of her mind to steal from him!— Who the hell gon' steal from my Titus an' survive?

BOB: How is Beatie?

MRS. SKINNER: Well, I heard she ain't too bad—ain't ripped up in the face—I don't know, the way the talk goes up an' down the street, what the hell should you believe? —He broke some ribs an' some other stuff an' she bein' treated at Receiving an' her momma don't need to act this is the first time Beatie Roscoe got herself kicked hard by some man. That girl, that girl when she *eleven years old* been in trouble, nobody better try to blame any of this on Titus—

BOB: (*impatiently*) Momma, what did you tell the police about this?

MRS. SKINNER: What police? No police hung around, no police was after me.

BOB: Didn't the doctors say nothin'?—about Mason?

MRS. SKINNER: I don't know, I don't know if it was a doctor come by or not—that place too big an' mixed-up—somebody came on by an' was in a hurry to fix Mason up an' I told him it was a accident, some hot water spilled out in the kitchen, or something like that, an' the man don't ask no questions about it because he got work to do. I don't interfere with them, they on their own an' I on my own. Mason, he quiet all the time. *He* real brave. He was sayin' to me, *Momma, don't tell the police or Titus either, please Momma, please*—

BOB: (*contemptuously*) *He* is really crazy, thinkin' Titus won't know about this!

MRS. SKINNER: (*sympathetically*) Now you right, honey, you right, you *very* right, but ... but we don't want to agitate Mason right now.... He's got it in his head to be afraid of them all. Earl an' Rollie that did it to him, but also the police, and also his own brother ... he all mixed-up, but I ain't got the heart to tell him. Titus, now, Titus ain't no angel, I am not claiming that ... got a worse temper than his father did ... but (*becoming proud*) ... but one thing you got to say, Titus is his own self, he is into the economy an' makin' that economy *work*—he is not hangin' around on the street or shootin' needles in himself—Clara Roscoe, now, she been on welfare the last ten years an' got no shame, an' her girl Beatie is just a whore, an' her son Conroy, why Conroy aged a old man, aged fifty years the last time I seen him—he very *sick* with drugs an' no kind of pride—an' her boy Earl, why Earl is goin' to be—

BOB: Momma, you did so good not tellin' the police anything— Momma, that was so sharp— If Titus come home an' found that out, that you went to the police an' not to him—why—Titus be heartbroke—

SCENE FOUR

A storage room. TITUS, *dressed as in Scene 1, is standing with one foot on* EARL, *who lies on his side with his hands bound together.* ROLLIE *is on the floor nearby, sitting awkwardly; his hands are also bound. Both boys are dressed shabbily and there are blood-stains on the front of* EARL's *shirt. Slide:* TRACEY *and* MORRIS, TITUS's *friends, looming in the background.*

TITUS: (*in a lordly, musical, farcical voice*) You scared boys, ain't you? Scared? Scared as hell? Ain't you? Got a real purpose to bein' scared, you bring Titus Skinner back from a high-level deal three hundred miles away.... Only good luck for you boys I am in a party mood from some handsome negotiations. Earl Roscoe, you, you look up when I talk. Ain't you in a frenzy, now? (*prods* EARL, *who holds himself rigid*) you just puttin'-on to be brave. I know. I know niggers like you inside an' out. I known your slut sister Beatie inside an' out the first time I got within a yard of her, an' your drunk momma ain't much improvement, an' your brother Conroy rotting on his feet—been on his bad sick habit far before *my* time in the trade— Ain't my connection, none of it, I just laugh at it. I just laugh. Earl, boy, you payin' close attention to me...? You respecting my words...?

(EARL *manages to look up at* TITUS. *This immediately pleases him; he withdraws his foot and squats down between* EARL *and* ROLLIE.)

TITUS: (*seriously, more 'naturally'*) How she comin' along, boy?

EARL: She okay.

TITUS: Took to a doctor, or what?

EARL: ...down to the hospital...they been fixin' her up...got some stuff...some tape on her....

TITUS: What, broke ribs?

(EARL, *sullenly, does not reply.* TITUS *pauses, as if contemplating something.*)

TITUS: I maybe gon' pay the bills; I got connections with some real doctor, what they call a *internist....* That a real doctor, that you never seen around here, a real expensive doctor you can't just contact walkin' in off the street...lots of them in the city if you know how to find them. (*laughs*) There is lots of surprisin' things, boy, all over the city, lots of things niggers like you never get hold of.... That ain't the first time you' sister got worked over, was it?

EARL: You never had no right—

ROLLIE: (*to* EARL, *desperately*) Shut up!

TITUS: Look, *her* face better off than my brother Mason's, ain't it?

EARL: We don't know nothin' about that—

TITUS: Nothin' about what?

EARL: Somethin' said to happen to you' brother, we heard the talk all over, we never—

TITUS: I hear the news a long distance away. I ain't even got time to check it. I act very fast, you got to be impressed how fast I check back here. But I come back to one surprise: that you two boys is still in town.

ROLLIE: We don't know nothin' about Mason—

EARL: No, I only got the news from—

TITUS: No, no, you handlin' you'selves bad as Beatie, you boys *can't lie worth a damn.* (*laughs, straightens and becomes more musical again in his speech*) Serve you right, you boys, somebody come along an' fix up you' handsome faces like my brother's—that got to be a sight, a spectacle— Howcome you gone after Mason? Mason ain't no significance. Howcome you never tried for me myself?...Oh, you is enjoyin' such luck that Titus Skinner is in a party mood, made some top-drawer connections on the map! *Not no map you ever seen!* Damn if anybody on that map ever heard about Beatie or Mason or any such shit, not nothin', points out to you how much it matters— It don't matter, it don't matter what happen down here in this neighborhood, it don't matter one shit, you got that? *It don't matter.* Ain't nobody interested. The man call me in an' I think to myself, *Titus, he gon' write you off the list!* But he never heard or gave no goddam about Beatie nor any of my personal business, he got high plans for me instead, he told me, *Titus, got high plans for you, been shiftin' an' arrangin' personnel, an' we ready for some promotion upward anytime you ready....* You understandin' any of this?

EARL: (*cautiously*) Howcome you drug us in here—?

TITUS: Howcome you think?

EARL: You think we did somethin' to Mason an'—

TITUS: But you innocent, huh? You both innocent?

EARL: Yeah, we innocent—

TITUS: (*laughing*) You victims of a severe miscalculation, you think I give one damn about Mason—*Mason Skinner*—he ain't my brother, not that half-ass. He ain't *nothin'.* I don't contend my mind with him. (*makes a contemptuous gesture*) Look, I on the business-scale. I playin' the open market— you know what that is? Open market? Economy market? You understand words like that? (EARL *and* ROLLIE *appear baffled.*) This minute, you is all lookin' at a individual headed for the future! I goin' to soar upward with the spiral, ain't nothin' to stop me! All of life an' stuff you boys never heard of is goin' up, it's growin' up, upward, you follow that? It's a bulgin' to make things grow, like plants comin'— uh — carrots an' trees—things down in the ground, that insist on their way *up.* That natural. That the *natural law.* A whole place —a city —a nation—is constructed similar—it goes up—the fast-thinkin' boys is like trees themselves an' they break loose an' go up with it an' they is saved—(TITUS *pauses, as if a little embarrassed by his mysticism, then squats down again beside* EARL *and seizes his hair.*) Hey, you is a familiar face, you, boy, you is a smart little motherfucker, ain't you? You is just the size of all them smart little niggers applyin' for jobs with me, with Titus Skinner. You is, you is just the size! You tell me one fact, Earl: did you' big-mouth momma call the police on me?

EARL: No—

TITUS: Didn't call no police?

EARL: No, she never—

TITUS: That a wise, important fact. (*nods*) Yes, boy, that a miracle-fact for you.... When you get back to you' momma, you instruct her she did right, an' you' Beatie the same. Some of them police hangin' on me too close.... Hey, you, Earl, hey, hey.... Is you sorry you messed up Mason's ugly face?

EARL: I never—

TITUS: Look, he only a half-brother! He don't count! (*laughs*) How-come you boys messed up Mason's ugly face, messed-up bad enough before! (*seriously*) I don't trust Mason. He got the sad, sad heart, he always lookin' at me an' thinkin' some thought I can't get to. He nothin' but a garbage man but he got this...this... (*vaguely*) He got this look to his face, only now he ain't got no face, the news I heard, no face left.... All that a very strange business, very complicated to think about.... (TITUS *breaks out of this spell and walks around energetically*.) Now look, I gon' pro-nounce sentence on you boys. I like one of them judges downtown. I calculatin' all the odds an' back-an'-forth an' come to this thought: two husky boys makin' a mistake, what's the crime to society of that mistake? Got to weigh it all. On one hand I got to deal punishment, on the other hand I got to calculate. But, you know how the street is—all up an' down the street they watchin', they lookin' to see what Titus gon' do now. Howcome you' sweet sister got her ass broke—I got a reputation most precarious to maintain— You' brother Conroy got hands on certain merchandise of mine an' he ain't anywhere in town an' I got my main interest in him— Where's Conroy hidin'?

EARL: I got no connection with Conroy—

TITUS: Where is he?

EARL: Jesus, Conroy might be dead—I don't know—I got no con-nection—

ROLLIE: Conroy ain't been seen—

TITUS: You think he is gone, he is out of town for good?

EARL: —got no connection with Conroy—

TITUS: You boys thought you was a television show, draggin' my half-ass brother away like that. Look here. (*takes a coin out of his pocket*) I gon' give you a lesson in floatin' currency. Like: a coin is worth fifty cents, but it is also worth nothin'. It ain't nothin', no nourishment. It ain't nothin', but it's worth fifty cents.... That's

my reputation. I come up the difficult way, I did my grubbin' an'
never laid back, *I* not a welfare shithead like the rest of you niggers,
an' I ain't no garbage man neither, nor anything classifiable on the
records (*proudly*) when them records is goin' to be written up....
So, boys, I gon' put a proposition to you.

(TITUS*'s manner is clever, cruel, a self-consciousness so total as to
be almost mystic, egoless, as if he were the author not only of his
own words but of the entire scene.*)

TITUS: This coin here is you' Fate. You believe in Fate? O.K. I gon' toss
this coin in the prescribed manner an' give you heads-or-tails
choice of it, an' no trick to it, for I am above common trickery. You
call it heads an' if it is heads, why, why I gon' release you an' shake
hands eye-to-eye, that my privilege, to raise up two black boys that
is good promisin' material.... That my privilege an' my power in
life, when I stand lookin' down at the shit laid all over this city
that is *you*. But, but now, but on the other hand, now, there is a
fact of life not so easy, that don't have the happy endin' like on
television, that you boys is got to realize and that fact of life is
makin' a mistake when you call the coin. Like, like you name it
heads an' it turn out *tails*. That must be taken in stride. You got
that? So you boys make the wrong mistake an' you in the hands of
Fate an' cryin' out for corrective procedure. (*He unscrews the cap
on a can of kerosene.*) Hey, Jesus, this-here stuff *strong!* This goes
right up into you' head an' clears it out! This-here good stuff,
Grade-A guaranteed stuff, no questions asked, no money-back.
Earl, honey, what your opinion on this—?

(*He holds the can so that* EARL *can smell it;* EARL, *terrified, says
nothing.*)

TITUS: You, Rollie? You just a sad-faced nigger, ain't you? You just not
assimilatin' all this, ain't you? (*holds it for* ROLLIE *to smell*) Now,
here is the deal: the punishment gon' be Chinese style, how they do
over there. You seen them pictures in the paper?—the monks or
whatever they are, how they burn them up? They step out of line
one inch an' they is *burned* up, no questions asked, that the rule
of the law over there, them, uh, Buddhists or whatever they is ... I
forget which one does the thing, which side is which, but it *effective*
in the public eye, an' points out how nobody don't need to take no
shit from nobody, which is my philosophy also. I got a better style

than dumpin' some hot water on a poor bastard's head, you got to admit. (*like an impresario, or a magician*) So, I gon' toss my coin, that I have faith in. You, boys, (*to slide of* TRACEY *and* MORRIS) you stand right up close to be impartial witnesses, there is *no* trickery involved in Titus Skinner, I gon' be fair like the Statue of Liberty itself holdin' the scales both ways, no prejudice. Now you don't let down you' momma an' the other folks waitin' for you, this is a important moment in you' life, beginnin' a whole new career with Titus Skinner or gettin' burnt up alive in two minutes.... Boy, you remember one thing: there is a universal lesson here, an' it don't matter which way you choose, you learnt the lesson inside-out.... You ready? (*He tosses the coin, it rolls on the floor, he steps on it and stands waiting.*)

SCENE FIVE

A darkened stage, which slowly lights up to reveal BEATIE, *seated on a folding chair, and the* PROSECUTOR, *a white man, who is standing.*

PROSECUTOR: Beatie, I'm sorry to keep this up, I wish I could let you go home ... but I think you know that justice has got to be done now. You realize it, don't you? You can't protect murderers like Titus Skinner any longer. You've got to recognize that these murderers are killing *you* ... killing your kind ... I mean your families, your brothers. It isn't a question of protecting innocent people. Beatie? Miss Roscoe? Will you answer my questions?

BEATIE: (*in a daze*) It was all this commotion down on the street ... an' I got Momma out of bed ... it was, oh, it was maybe four in the mornin' ... an' I heard the noises ... they was people makin' noise. ...

PROSECUTOR: It was 4:25 A.M.

BEATIE: An' my God I put on some clothes an' run down there ... I see my friend Lana goin' down ahead of me an' I called out, I asked her what it was, an' she said she don't know, she was goin' down just in her pajamas.... (*laughs*) Lana is real wild, she a crazy one, but close to my heart ... she my own age by two weeks.... So I run down front with her an' these people yellin' out on the sidewalk, an' we got there, an' these two.... (*pauses*) These two boys ...

bodies.... There was these.... People was runnin' up from all over an' sayin', *Look here!* an' I could smell how it was somethin' burnt like meat...an' Lana an' me got there, an' there was these...these two....

(*She falls silent. The* PROSECUTOR *is very sympathetic.*)

BEATIE: Well...they was all burned.... It was both of them, they was all burned.... Out on the sidewalk front of our place. Somebody asked Momma, *Where you' boy, Earl—he up in bed or what?* Somebody said, *That look like Earl, that one.* They was arguin' about it. Then I got mixed-up an' had to be put somewhere.... I no longer got a stable constitution; I gettin' bad as Momma. (*laughing*) Momma not herself all the time. She come round, she apologize how wild she been actin', down here, actin' so crazy an' tryin' to kick an' bite you.... She don't mean no harm but is gone off her head. When I was beat-up she took good care of me, she cried an' said, she said this was exactly what she expect, from me tailin' around Titus Skinner. But she didn't go wild with it, because I was not hurt bad...an' he never messed up my face.... She took good care of me, she a very loving mother when it necessary. But.... But with Earl.... With Earl it kind of pointless.... It kind of pointless...to be a loving mother...or anything else.... You could not tell Earl from Rollie, that was a confusion. Some white man was askin' me to identify my brother, an' he laid stress on the clothes aspect of it, like shoes that was left, but Jesus (*in amazement*) they was alike.... So if you wanted to grieve for one you would grieve for the other.... I get mixed-up. Like a face...a face is what tells us apart, ain't it? (*She looks at the* PROSECUTOR, *who nods with compassion but does not answer her question.*) I mean a face...on the outside, here...a face is the way you tell people apart, an' people who ain't you? It is the method, ain't it? (*She leans around in her chair to appeal to unseen others.*) What the difference between us, if there ain't no face left? (*wildly*) Oh I gon' get more mixed-up, raked around in my brains...like my poor Momma.... I gon' get sick if somebody don't spell out some answers to me.... (*after a pause, more calmly*) Well they got no face left, that's a fact. Somebody took pictures of them. But none for the newspaper up close, it was too nasty, they don't print the pictures like that. They take them, though. (*vaguely*) All goin' into the record...into the book....

(The PROSECUTOR *leafs through his notes, carefully.)*

PROSECUTOR: This all began, Beatie, when you took several hundred dollars' worth of narcotics from Titus Skinner's room?

BEATIE: *(vaguely)* ...It's bein' writ down, somebody takin' notes an' recordin' it.... The answers to the question's right there, no mix-up to it....

PROSECUTOR: Beatie ...? Can you answer my question, please? This all began when you stole five hundred dollars' worth of heroin from Titus Skinner's room on 119th Street, is that an accurate representation of the truth? Or would you like to modify it?

BEATIE: Earl always a loud boy, but nice to me.... Since he ten, eleven, a real little kid he stayin' away from where we lived.... I don't know that Rollie real well. But he was bad company for Earl, them two boys bad on each other... too soft-flexible... takin' stuff, runnin' around the street high-up.... Momma give up on him long time ago like she give up on Conroy....

PROSECUTOR: Your brother, Conroy, asked you to steal the narcotics, didn't he? That's what we've heard, from reliable sources. Where is Conroy?

BEATIE: The evil eye put it to me ... lookin' at me.... Conroy, he so sick an' messy, his arms all shrunk-up ... got the evil eye inside him, in his head an' lookin' out. I was feelin' so good. I was feelin' high-up myself, the way Titus made a fuss around me an' bought me some stuff... bought me a coat an' some boots.... A fur coat.... The boots was white leather an' made by hand, cost seventy-five dollars from Saks.... I got mixed-up in my own mind, how far I could go with Titus. He was actin' so foolish over me that I... I made a mistake.... Conroy put the thought to me, to take some package or somethin' that wouldn't be noticed, just some package, a bag of somethin', when Titus had a lot of it, an' maybe wouldn't notice.... Conroy so sick, he so crazy off his head.... So I mishandled some item from... *(pause)* a problematical person.

PROSECUTOR: At which point Titus Skinner beat you up. Right? And then your brother and a friend of his tortured Mason Skinner, is that correct? And Titus Skinner, to retaliate, kidnapped and murdered your brother and his friend. Yes, we know all this, it's clear and predictable. *(He looks around.)* We were able to predict, almost to the hour, when the bodies would be found....

BEATIE:... Long time before the commotion out front, all that night I
been havin' these off-an'-on dreams... bad dreams..... I felt very
electric. I known Earl was up to somethin', that was the talk. Then
later I got the news on Mason Skinner. So I known it all. I was just
waitin'. Downtown they give me some pills, so I could sleep, but
anyway I was wakin' up an' my mouth tasted so rotten.... I felt
all jumpy like with electric sparks. Momma, she was so drunk, laid
down with all her clothes on an' snored right off, but I more sensi-
tive an' was put to the torture, them dreams I had. I think there is
too much electric power loose in a city this size. If people bein'
careless take the plugs out of the sockets on the wall, why, it stands
to reason... it stands to logical reason... that electricity would get
loose an' into the air.... An' you multiply that by millions people
an' you see what a thing it is.... One time there was a story in the
Sunday paper on the electric chair, that they used to use here in
state, but decided against, an' there was pictures of it, an' I showed
a picture of it to Earl—he was maybe fifteen then—an' I said to
Earl, *So you ain't gon' wind up in this chair after all!* They got it
in a museum or somethin' now. So Earl said, *No, I got to leave this
state for that privilege.* I didn't get these words. But, but later I did,
I think I did, later other things come to help me, an' I half-known
what he meant. Like, like you are out walkin' on the street in open
daylight an' you think to you'self, all at once: *What if I run out in
front of that bus?* I have seen a shadow self of Beatie Roscoe do
such a thing. I know. Earl had the electricity in him, all jumps an'
sparks. Couldn't make use of it. They said him an' Rollie did some
hard thing to Mason Skinner, an' maybe so, maybe not, I never
checked out the information. But if so it was the electricity done it,
jumpin' out of Earl, to turn him so nervous an' mean like he been
the last few years.... He worse than Conroy, even. Conroy always
been mean but not out-of-the-way mean, if you wasn't in his way,
he not goin' to run over you. Earl different, Earl too excitable.
There is a lesson in it... but I don't know what it is.

PROSECUTOR: Beatie...? You'll testify for us, won't you? You'll be a
witness against him?

BEATIE: Who? Against who?

PROSECUTOR: You know who. *Titus Skinner.*

BEATIE: Which one that...? Look here. (*She stands, opens the top of
her dress, so that the welts on her back can be seen.*) An' around
back here on my head... there is awful aches an' seizures, from

where he pounded me on the floor. Used up every pimp trick he known, on me, beatin' me where it don't show, for protection of the product.... It's a razor-edge, how mad they get...a man when he starts beatin' on you...unless his mind's in perfect poise, like Titus's, he could go too far an' mash the face in.

PROSECUTOR: You need only tell us the truth, and stick to your story, and we'll protect you and your mother and your brother, we'll take every precaution.... Beatie, you've agreed?

BEATIE: Wish I hadn't been so sick, so bad-feelin', I could maybe gone over to Mason Skinner's an' talked to him...him an' me, we got along O.K., he a nice guy, he not like the other Skinners that they would spit in you' eye if they could.... Oh Jesus, if it'd been Mason Skinner instead of Titus, that I got so high on.... I got to see that man face-to-face an' make a sense of all this. You put Titus Skinner away, it don't matter, he got control of things an' make life miserable for people. They all scared of him, don't like him but they scared of him, like worship him, they don't want to get killed like my brother.... All this is complex behavior. I ain't equipped to deal with it. But somebody got to deal with it... (*vaguely*) got to make a sense of it an' get it reduced to a word you can understand....

PROSECUTOR: Is that word going to be *yes*...? (*waits patiently, while* BEATIE *shakes her head slowly, as if not understanding him*) Yes, Beatie, is it *yes*...? We'll protect you and your family. We know exactly how to handle this. Titus Skinner is a marked man — we've got warrants out for him and we'll get him in a few hours! He's been arrested eight times and he's always gotten away, he's squirmed out of assault charges, nighttime theft charges, possession of narcotics charges, but this time it's first-degree homicide. That bastard was making four thousand a week, I happen to know! *Four thousand a week!*... You can help us out, Beatie, Titus Skinner was your lover for a period of six to eight weeks, and you are well-informed about him. We'll be extremely grateful to you. What do you say?

BEATIE: (*uncertainly*) Somebody was my *lover*...? Somebody loved me...? When was that...?

PROSECUTOR: Are you going to testify on our side? Are you going to cooperate?

BEATIE: What was that you said, what word...? You said...?

PROSECUTOR: We'll keep you and your family in custody, Beatie, in protective custody out of town, in another city.... *Are you going to cooperate?*

BEATIE: ...Too late by now anyway, he put his mark on me. Not on my face but everywhere else. I used up. I all used up. Sixteen years old goin' on nothin'....

PROSECUTOR: (*turns off recorder*) That means *yes,* then. I assume that means *yes.*

BEATIE: Might as well be.... Yes. Yes, I will testify. Yes. I used up anyhow, might as well keep goin'. *Yes.*

PROSECUTOR: (*perfunctory now*) And we'll protect you, Beatie. You'll be absolutely safe until the trial and during the trial, and we promise a conviction.... We're going to stop this kind of lawlessness and make this city safe for everyone, regardless of color or race.

SCENE SIX

KIDD, *the white defense attorney, an attractive man in his mid-thirties, is pacing and speaking excitedly before the* JUDGE, *an older white man whose image is projected. Off to the left, at a table, sits* TITUS, *dressed in a cheap, "respectable" suit.*

KIDD: (*very moved*) ...Your Honor, for one thing...for one thing the police acted without legitimate reason to suspect the men they arrested...they were acting out of hatred, ignorant hatred.... Your Honor, they got a search warrant on flimsy evidence, I have reason to suspect that they acted solely on the word of a police informer...an enemy of Titus Skinner's...someone who wants to see Titus in trouble.... Your Honor, my client's life has been threatened often in the past, and it was simply for reasons of self-protection that he had the weapons the police seized, in his car... and the narcotics they claim to have discovered, in a room rented under the name of Skinner, Your Honor, Your Honor I submit that the narcotics were *not* the property of any of these men here before you this morning, they claim absolute ignorance of any narcotics whatsoever.... Your Honor, I am not accusing the police of having planted this evidence. I am only accusing them...I am trying to make you see, Your Honor, make you *see....* Your Honor, if you will look again at the record, you will see that Titus

Skinner, aged twenty-nine, has *never* been convicted of a serious crime. His earliest arrests were for misdemeanors ... petty thefts ... he spent eight months in the detention home, and his probation officer, Mr. Hough, indicated, Your Honor, indicated that Titus was one of the more responsible boys at the Home ... and that his year of probation was without incident.... Your Honor, all this took place twelve years ago, and since then my client has been arrested but *not* convicted of the charges brought against him by the police.... Your Honor, I am going to move that all these charges be dropped, since the evidence is patently flimsy and it is an outrage—

JUDGE: (*on tape*) Motion denied.

KIDD: Your Honor, the charges of first-degree homicide, these charges are without precedent on such transparent evidence—the prosecution is in possession of certain witnesses I insist upon meeting with—I insist upon a meeting with all the witnesses—I insist upon a realization of the horror of this act, this search-and-seize warrant issued from this very room, on make-shift evidence, distortions brought about by racial hatred, deeply-felt unconscious or conscious urges toward genocide—in evidence everywhere in our environment, and I do not exclude the law-enforcement officers of our city, I do not accuse but I do not exclude, the record of the courts, the record of poorly disguised racial bigotry in the form of judicial procedure—I am entering a plea for—

JUDGE: (*on tape*) Denied.

KIDD: —for a reduction of the charges— (*As if their timing is off,* KIDD *glances at the* JUDGE, *then resumes.*) I am requesting a reduction of the charges from first-degree homicide to manslaughter.

JUDGE: (*on tape*) Denied.

KIDD: I am requesting bail for my clients, reasonable bail to allow them to return to their families, Your Honor. I request bail for these young men on the basis, Your Honor, that the prosecution has no witnesses for the alleged crime, has put together a shabby and outrageous case, has no real case, is acting out of hostility and not compassion, it is all hearsay, it is simple street gossip, Your Honor, despicable, shameful, vengeful impulses from the gutter.... I request, may it please Your Honor, total cognizance of the humanity of these healthy young men, imprisoned beneath ceilings much too low for their height, shackled like dangerous animals, beasts denied their full humanity by a racist society—young men bewildered and terrified *at this very moment* by their surroundings, their isolation, their heritage from the days of slavery, their crowded conditions, their poor schooling, black genes, their ravenous bellies, their anguished starving souls starving for existence—I plead in their behalf—I declare—I insist that they are innocent as we are all innocent, under the law of our nation, we are all innocent until someone somewhere tracks us down and arrests us and proves in open—open—court how we are guilty, and causes to be brought in against us in open court, in absolute openness, by a jury of our peers, causes to be brought in against us, all of us, a verdict of *Guilty....* Your Honor, (*He speaks passionately, wildly.*) Your Honor, until that day...until that hour...we are innocent and my clients are innocent...we are all innocent under the law until that verdict is handed down.... And so, and so...and so I... (*He pauses. After a moment he approaches the bench and speaks more calmly, normally.*) I request that my clients be released on bail.

JUDGE: (*on tape*) Denied.

(KIDD *considers this. Slide of* JUDGE *off.* KIDD *approaches* TITUS.)

KIDD: He was touched, he was very moved. I saw it. He was very moved. Did you see it? I saw it. He's up for re-election and has to be cagey, though. But I saw it, I felt it. Didn't you? Didn't you feel it? I'm very confident....

TITUS: What happened? What went on? What was all that shit? Somebody more gon' get killed, somebody gon' be annihilated all over this shithead town—I want a change of venue! (TITUS *grabs* KIDD *and is about to strike him, then stalks out instead.*) I want some new attorney's got some knowledge-about-town, not no preacher crap-head, I want my money back, I'm entering a plea to be my own attorney an' the hell with everybody else—

KIDD: (*calling after him, idealistically and yet half-mockingly*) We touched him—we made an impression—justice will be done—don't lose confidence—don't lose faith in America—

SCENE SEVEN

A bare stage, onto which CONROY ROSCOE *walks. He is shabbily dressed, appears much older than his real age of thirty-one, and his sense of self—of a confined ego—is minimal. He is in a state of perpetual terror, which is interrupted or relieved by half-human states of awareness, cunning, practicality, even a kind of humor. (He is not a* symbol *of anything; he is, or was, a conscious human being who has been altered into something both larger and smaller than his specific "self.")*

CONROY: (*peering around, frightened; is aware of the audience*) Where is this? Is this St. Louis? I was headed there...I was meant to go there...but if I got here instead I was meant to get here.... They got the police after me, I know the police is huntin' me down...or huntin' somebody down that looks like me...the way I looked... I...uh...But I a sick man, no threat, I not askin' for mercy but only justice...to be let alone to die...to ask of you the patience, the kind patience, to be given the normal amount of time to die, that in my case the doctor said was, uh, two-three years he stated, unless something speeded it up...which he also stated... (*shakes head in amusement*) Oh Jesus, he a nice young guy, he scairt as hell just to see me, he shook up, he say to me like in a whisper *You're dying!* I was sick that day but not so sick to lose my dignity, so I said to him, he was a white kid an' scairt of how I got the shudders, I said *So are you!*—an' it shook him up the more, to notice I had a operatin' brain. But it ain't operatin' to do damage, it ain't operatin' at full-function, don't you hold that against me! —I no harm to you, I not a threat or problem— (*stares at audience*) I lookin' in a dark place an' the dark place lookin' back at me. It don't speak. It waitin' for me to make the false move. (*After a moment he seems to re-assert himself as* CONROY.) ...No...No, I am Conroy, I am the one, yes, if you lookin' for him, but, the fact is, this is the fact, the fact is I am very sick an' my memory is gone an' it was maybe somebody set down an' argued with me an' said I am named Conroy an' got it drummed an' shouted into my head so I gave in an' said *All right! I'm Conroy!*—so you let me alone an' stop shoutin' at me! That might of happened; last night or some other night. I been loose for a long time. I been on the run for my life.... But I known you would catch up to me.... (*peers at audience*) You ain't no friends of Titus...? Titus, he very mean, he very famous-mean, I would not go against Titus, no, not if I was crazy even, never.... Titus beyond me. I ain't in his way. I am innocent. I goin' to lay down off to the side not on the sidewalk, an' I ain't in any of you' way, I ain't no trouble to you.... How-come my little brother got himself killed, it ain't part of my curio-sity, I too sick, but I believe he made the choice. You can't stop them, the young kids. They is already too wild for my generation. I heard he was burned up by a match, but I don't pay attention to such shit, that just nigger-talk an' speculatin' an' I too sick for it an' so far out of town an' it ain't even clear if I am Conroy or if somebody, some black bastard, talked me into that name an' walked off free himself.... All my life I been dedicated to my own explanation, that took me a long time to figure out. I always on the *search*. I searchin' for the famous powder, that you put it into a liquid an' a needle an' into the blood, an' it make you magic... like God.... I dedicated to that search, I very dedicated an' worn out with years of it... I always gettin' news that somebody got the real thing to deal me, the new formula, an' I got the faith in it, an' always ready, an' ain't found it yet...but when they invent it, I gon' be first customer, I gon' rush in there no matter how sick I am.... Now I pretty bad, I goin' to pieces fast. I recognize this. But even if I layin' down in the street half dead when they make the discovery, even then I gon' jump up an' get in the front of the line, to get that powder.... I am a inflatable deflatable balloon. I am in the shape of a man, a black man, but it a balloon in that shape, an' I in charge of blowin' the balloon up, an' then it leak out the air by itself, slow, until I is flat to nothin' an' got to start hustlin' again to blow myself up.... That a daily task, in fact a four-times-a-day task. When I was stronger I could hustle twelve-fourteen hours a day, now I a little sick, but I try for the full workday, I dedicated to the problem an' willin' to work hard every day, that mean *every day*, no Saturday-Sunday off, or special Monday holi-day, no vacation in the summer or anytime, I don't never rest my ass moren a few hours. ... But I ninety years old now in the insides, an' the doctor say my guts is shrivel up all over, an' that got the solid force of science behind it, a forecast like that, so, so if you is concerned about *me* (*laughs*) you is mistaken...because I ain't goin' to harm you or nobody in you' family.... Long as I last, I goin' to be a out-of-the-way man. I a good customer of people like Titus, I pour money into the pockets of the economy, I don't ask for money-back, for guarantee, for repair-work or realignment or recyclin' or nothin' of that nature, because the product I buy is never open to doubt.... If you tryin' to get me back home for the police, why, why I in no condition to testify, I all confused an' no-good. I am fast disappearing. I am a dyin' man an' take it in stride ... I am not a complainer... I am always a good customer an' no troublemaker whether I am in my own mind or somebody else's. ... I only plead innocent, I no harm to you, I no threat... I am dyin' of innocence....

SCENE EIGHT

A street in front of the Skinners' house.

MRS. SKINNER: Look here (*extends hands*) how I am shakin', I am shakin' in an' out just like this—you know that son of a bitch Herman—

BOB: Momma, what the hell—

MRS. SKINNER: You listen! That Herman, that big black son' bitch, he bump into me in the drugstore an' say to me, how Titus goin' be sent up for damn sure this time, an' once he out of the way all the Skinners better haul themselves out of here—

BOB: Herman told you that? *Herman?*

MRS. SKINNER: He say lots of people is holdin' back, what they goin' to do—oh, he was drunk an' shootin' off his mouth, but he was tellin' the truth—I am just shakin', I am so nervous of all this— An' he tryin' to postpone that trial, that Mr. Kidd, he always tryin' to change things around, the court schedule all mixed-up to high heaven—

BOB: Howcome Herman got it in for us? Titus ain't never—

MRS. SKINNER: Not just Herman! They all fed up, they waitin' like cats in the alley for somethin' to be tossed out, somethin' dead, they just gloatin' an' talkin' so free about Titus—now you know they *never*—

BOB: Well, Titus ain't hauled off yet. Titus got a very good chance—

MRS. SKINNER: You know they *never* talkin' so free before—in fact they was necessarily on my side, 'gainst Beatie's Momma—they all tellin' me how Titus known how to treat that little bitch—she so stuck-up thinkin' she pretty—now they is all lookin' at me, I'm afraid to go down onto the sidewalk—

BOB: Mason ain't no damn help to you, layin' there like that—Jesus, I so sick of tryin' to hammer some sense in that brain of his.... He actin' weird all the time...he got a long hatred for Titus, he ain't goin' to admit it to you nor anybody, he just damn don't want Titus to get free.

SCENE NINE

MASON: I remember that I went to school!...yes, that was me, I think it was me...wasn't that me? Mason Skinner? Back a long time ago...uh...he was very small and scared...I can see him...I remember...he went up front of the room on the last day of school, all the kids were dressed up an' had their poems to recite, an' he went up front an' the teacher then—it was a woman—the teacher said *O.K., now Mason, everybody quieted down now an' ready*— So he said the poem right off—

God appears and God is light
To those poor souls who dwell in night
But does a human form display
To those who dwell in realms of day.

He said it right off...he didn't make a mistake...I think... (*pause*) Then I betrayed everybody's confidence, the tax-payers lost faith in me, or somebody like me, maybe my brother did some bad things with schoolbooks, that the tax-payers bought an' provided me with...or somebody like me.... Which one of them was it? I got a lot of brothers. Jesus, I got so many of them...they are anxious to lean hard on me...dump boiling water over my head ...make sure it is sweetened with sugar to make it stick to the skin an' not run off.... Earl Roscoe, who is now dead, did a thing to my face that woke me up hard: now I am tryin' to get back to who I am, which one of them. I am maybe Earl, myself. I could be Earl... I could be Earl, or Mason, or Titus, or Conroy...any of them...I got to analyze it out, if only I could have some quiet. But there is this racket, this commotion...bangin' on the ceiling and the walls an' yellin' down in the street...an' people up close to me, crowdin' an' yellin' like all my life...I got to sanctify the space around me (*indicates space around his body*) but I got to do it myself, it is a hard task...it is askin' a lot....

SCENE TEN

The Skinner living room. MASON *lying on the sofa.* MRS. SKINNER *enters with* KIDD.

MRS. SKINNER: Mr. Kidd, here is my son Mason. He very sharp, the sharpest one— Mason, this is Mr. Kidd, that you' brother got retained for the trial—he just wants to talk to you an' ask some things—

KIDD: Titus is certainly going to get free—there's no question about it. He'll be acquitted. It's only a matter of the means we use to get the acquittal—I want to use every possible means—

MASON: He goin' to request me to be a character witness, I know that, well, I ain't goin' to make no public appearance in no courtroom, that a final fact. Howcome that television off? I watchin' the show —(*sneering*) Momma say I the sharpest one of the boys, she means I got the good grades in school, which is a truth, but I turnin' my back on that shit, an' I concentratin' on the television—I got nothin' to say to you, Mr. Kidd.

KIDD: Mason, I only want to—

MASON: Howcome I *Mason* to you so fast?

MRS. SKINNER: Mason, you bein' damn rude!

KIDD: (*embarrassed, awkward; then cleverly*) I think of you as Mason, because your brother speaks of you that way...and your mother, of course...and in my thoughts, when I think of you, I naturally think of *Mason*. But you're quite right, I shouldn't presume any intimacy with you. My own name is Harold—Harold Kidd. I only want to ask you a few questions—

MASON: (*his voice rising until it is shrill, mad*) I say that I livin' here in my own skin which is me, my own possession, an' I say you ain't gon' burn or cut it off me...nobody gettin' through that doorway to do it...there is a skeleton inside gon' fight you like hell, for the true ownership of that skin....

KIDD: (*to* MRS. SKINNER) What's wrong? What's happened to him?

MRS. SKINNER: Mason, he just goin' through a phase—a bad phase of his life— He very excitable, he don't take them pills like the prescription says to—

MASON: I'm in charge of myself! I can handle myself! I'm in sovereign control!

KIDD: Mason, I only want to help you and your family—I don't want to upset you— Believe me, please, this isn't just a job to me, this case isn't just an ordinary case, it has deep, terrible symbolic value —it goes far beyond itself and into history—

MASON: Don't you come near me!

KIDD: But I only want—

(BOB *enters*.)

MASON: These hands is not black or white or any color—these hands is on their own an' itchin' for somebody to rip—if somebody gets too close—

KIDD: Look, I know what you've gone through. I *know*. All your lives you people have been made to know that your birth, the color of your skin, is your fate—your skins are your fate—the shape of your lips is your *fate*— No one has ever looked at you, at your humanity— Do you think I don't know? Do you think all white men are blind to you?

MASON: I gon' skin you, hang it up on the door outside—I gon' defend myself inch by inch—outward mutilation if necessary—

BOB: (*shouting*) Jesus, Mason, you goin' crazy! You crazy-mouth, crazy shithead—

MASON: You an' him both stay away—I am warnin' you— Nobody's goin' get close to me again an' torture my face—I refuse it—I goin' defend every inch—

BOB: All this talk is just a way he got, a way he usin'—he wants Titus to get found guilty—he wants Titus to suffer—all this crazy-shit talk is just put-on.... (*He goes to* MASON, *tries to pull him up.* MASON *resists*.) All of us is goin' to talk for Titus—we goin' step up front at that courtroom—an' you goin' do you' share an' show you' goddam messed-up face—damn you—

MRS. SKINNER: Bob!

BOB: Momma, you to blame in this—you lettin' him lay here for a month—ain't had no bath, just lays there watchin' television— Momma, *he* ain't no worse off than anybody else—he just tryin' to die—

MRS. SKINNER: (*slaps him*) Little show-off snot! You goin' make a good appearance for Titus, ain't you—showin' off right now? You think this is the trial, this is the courthouse?—you showin' off in front of Mr. Kidd here? Well, Mr. Kidd he got better sense than to give any goddam about you' opinions— Get out of here an' let Mason alone.

BOB: If he don't do the right thing for Titus—if he let Titus down I goin' kill him myself an' finish the job— (*exits*)

MRS. SKINNER: Mr. Kidd, we goin' leave you two some privacy, to talk in peace. I sure am sorry for all this.... (*exits*)

(KIDD, *alone with* MASON, *looks at him, uneasily. For a while he doesn't speak. Nervously, he opens his briefcase and takes out some papers, leafs through them.* MASON *is lying back as if exhausted, one arm dangling down off the sofa. He is breathing hard.*)

KIDD: The trial is set now for October 11 ... I tried to get it postponed again but I couldn't ... but ... but I'm confident we'll win ... I'm confident.... But I need everyone's aid, I need character witnesses ... I need someone as articulate as yourself and ... and ... as tragic ... Mason? Can you hear me?

(KIDD *approaches* MASON, *slowly.* MASON *turns his head away, hardly an inch or so away, so that* KIDD *cannot meet his gaze.* KIDD *involuntarily touches his own face, gropingly, as if recoiling from* MASON's *deformity.*)

Mason, no one is going to hurt you. No one. Ever again.... My God, ... is that painful? ... your face ... ?

(*When* MASON *does not reply,* KIDD *speaks more normally.*)

Well, look. I'll get those boys acquitted, right here at home, the jury will see through the prosecution's flimsy case—not *one* eyewitness!—a discredited confession!—I'll demolish the prosecution's main argument, and it will give me great joy to do so.... Mason, you're listening, aren't you? Mason? I only want you to take the stand very briefly, to say just a few words on behalf of your brother ... to explain, uh, what kind of a brother he was ... did he buy things for you and your family, like, uh, things in this room

...and did he show affection for...(MASON *shudders and turns away, child-like.*) ...there's no risk involved. No risk. I know threats have been made against your family—even against me for defending your brother—but nothing will happen, no one will dare hurt us— (*proudly*) Threats have been made against me a half-dozen times in the past few years, but I haven't been intimidated. No one is going to intimidate *me*. Once I opened a package that came to me at my office—and it was a fake bomb—it was a cheap alarm clock tricked up to resemble a bomb—but a *fake* bomb, just to scare me—I was defending some conscientious objectors at the time— But the point is, the point is, the bomb was a *fake*—it was only meant to frighten me away— Most things are fakes when you examine them; they don't explode.

MASON: Leave me alone—

KIDD: No one is going to hurt you, Mason. (*pause*) The men who tortured you are dead.

MASON: (*looking around mockingly*) Who's dead? Where are they dead?

KIDD: Your torturers are dead—they're both dead—

MASON: Both?

KIDD: Both men.

MASON: Both? Both means *two*...?

KIDD: Yes, two. Two. They're both dead. They're *dead*.

MASON: *Two?*...There was a lot more than two of them....

KIDD: What?

MASON: I don't believe it. I want proof. I am never leavin' this place without absolute proof. Mr. Kidd, the whole universe better be dead before I riskin' it.

KIDD: Mason, if only you—

MASON: Who this *Mason* you always addressin'? He some brother to you, or somethin'? You know him by sight—or what? What's he look like, you so close to him?—you so easy with him?

KIDD: I'm sorry, I'm sorry if I—I'll call you Mr. Skinner—I—

MASON: Which one are you? (*confused*) I don't see the right way now... all the stuff is blurred, it all crooked an' sideways.... Howcome you in here, in my Momma's house?

KIDD: (*frightened*) Mason, my name is Harold Kidd...I'm your brother's attorney...(*After an awkward pause,* KIDD *walks away and begins a kind of speech, pacing around the room, excitedly, passionately; alternated with his speech is* MASON's *speech, which is delivered as he lies immobile.*)...my purpose is victory, another victory...another in a sequence of hard-fought hard-won victories...to be headlined everywhere, in all the newspapers... shouted everywhere in all the small towns...under the paving stones of the country.... A victory for your race, for the new dawn of this nation...for freedom, for justice, for *you*....

MASON: This place of my Momma's not secret enough to keep noises away. You got to burrow under the wallpaper to get safe. Or else they come trampin' in here—too many people—they turn off the television set an' start their own kind of television show an' the noise of it makes me awful nervous. When I get my own strength back, I goin' burrow under the wallpaper an' plaster an' stuff to find some peace.

KIDD:...I have a vision in which the Potomac overflows its banks ...and everything is mud, dense black evil mud, choking, suffocating everyone in its path...black mud like lava...a great mass without individual parts, without souls or faces...just an avalanche of mud...there will be no need for fire, for explosions... the mud will take everything before it...and...and the rest of us...men like myself...men with brains and maps of the future ...the rest of us will wait joyfully, we will guide and instruct and navigate the future.... Men have always been one-dimensional, except the men who write the history books! I plan on writing a book of my own, *my own*. I know what I'm doing. I can get the mud-flow started because...I don't think it's really going to happen...I mean, not *really*.... It couldn't really happen....

(KIDD *pauses, glances at* MASON, *who ignores him. He starts to leave, and* BOB *stops him in the hallway.*)

BOB: Hey—Mr. Kidd—you talked any sense in him?

KIDD: I'm absolutely confident—yes—I'm confident that your brother will come around to our way of thinking. We've been talking about many important things...the need for cooperation, for a united front...I'm confident it will turn out well.

BOB: You sure...? He goin' to be acquitted, you *sure?*

KIDD: Yesterday afternoon the defense committee received a check for $100,000. History is being made.

BOB: Uh...$100,000? Who gave you that much money?

KIDD: Gentle people, people who wish to remain anonymous, men of my race who are fierce that justice be done....

BOB: But who are they?

KIDD: Friends of yours. Friends of your brother's. Serious alarmed gentle people in this city....

BOB: Hey, I mean, who got $100,000 to give away? I mean...uh... howcome they got so much, to hand out like that? (KIDD *exits;* BOB *calls after him.*) Mr. Kidd? Hey, if I had what it takes to give away $100,000, I would give it away too...only I ain't got that much...only I am real happy an' thankful an' so is Titus, I speak for Titus here, an' all the rest of us...only I got this simple question: howcome there is somebody got so much he can give that much away...?

SCENE ELEVEN

Courtroom. BEATIE *is being examined by the* PROSECUTOR. *On her right, at his raised bench is the* JUDGE; *to her left, the jury box, with twelve white jurors seated in it, these men and women out of the light, dimly-seen. On the other side of the stage is the defense counsel's table, at which* TITUS *and* KIDD *sit; they too are out of the light.*

BEATIE:... Yes, that is right. Yes. Then he said to me, like he said a whole lot of times, he said, *Anytime anybody cross me, I got the where-abouts to take care of him.*

PROSECUTOR: Did Titus Skinner ever mention to you, or boast to you, that he had punished anyone in the past?

BEATIE: Yes, yes, that is right.... Yes. Yes, he did.... (*growing frightened*) Yes, I heard that. I heard something like that.

PROSECUTOR: Is it a fact that on the night of April 3 you were in the company of Titus Skinner?

BEATIE: (*slowly*) Yes...that was a day...that was a date....

PROSECUTOR: Would you speak more clearly, please, Miss Roscoe?

BEATIE: I think...yes...I think that was a date I remember, that something happened on....

PROSECUTOR: On the night of April 3, how would you describe Titus Skinner's behavior to you?

BEATIE: He...he said.... He....

(*A change comes over* BEATIE; *she begins to speak in fragments, in a tortuous manner, as if something were preventing her from speaking clearly. She is baffled, struggling to speak, but unable.*)

BEATIE:...then he said...he wanted.... (*after a pause*) I don't remember.

PROSECUTOR: (*stunned*) I beg your pardon?

BEATIE: I don't remember.

(*Everyone on stage shows some surprise; even the* JUDGE *glances down at* BEATIE, *for the first time.*)

PROSECUTOR: Miss Roscoe, I beg your pardon...? Were you answering my question...? I'll read you my question again and....

BEATIE: No, I don't remember. I don't think so. No. I don't think I was there.

PROSECUTOR: But Miss Roscoe, you were explaining to the court how, on the night of April 3, Titus Skinner took you to his room on West 119th Street, and—and you took from him, did you not, you took from him a quantity of heroin in a—

KIDD: Objection!

(SOUND: *gavel*)

PROSECUTOR: (*very upset, awkward; glances out at the audience, embarrassed*) I seem to be...I.... Your Honor, my witness is not well....

BEATIE: (*girlishly*) I am fine, I am in fine spirits! I am feelin' very fine!

PROSECUTOR: (*trying to resume his normal manner*) Miss Roscoe, will you go over the events of the night of April 3, please, to the best of your ability...?

BEATIE: What April 3? When? I don't remember it, I wasn't there. I don't know who it was there with him—he brought a girl back with him, yes, he was always hangin' on some girl— A big handsome son of a bitch—Titus Skinner—if that's who you are referring to— (*shocked; pretends to be surprised at her own words, looking around courtroom, then over at* TITUS) Jesus, I got to watch my mouth! I got a bad troublemakin' mouth! (*makes an effort to be serious, in a school-girlish manner*) But the fact is, you people that are listenin', I hope you are fully listenin', out there, the fact is this: a man got to trounce on a woman, an' if she hangs on him she's saying to him O.K. She's givin' to him that privilege. If she don't prefer that treatment she don't hang on him.... My Momma instructed me, she said, Beatie, if you drop out of that school—it was the LaMarvel Beauty College—if you violate that fifty-dollar tuition, then the hell with you, an' you better move right in with you' fancy boyfriend, 'cause I ain't havin' none of you. She made it clear enough. But. But I got my head all wild, the more I told them friends of mine an' the girls at the school how I was drivin' all over town with Titus Skinner, the more I talked the wilder I got, just in my head, and Jesus I got high on him!—so I thought why the hell keep down so low, just to learn how to shampoo people's heads that is too freaky lazy to do it themselves, an' white ladies givin' me dime tips, an' all that shit you got to take from a boss—why—then I was crossin' right over to a new life, an' Titus Skinner standin' there on the curb, waitin'. So. So, that happened that way.... So I made a cross-over, I made the decision. So I got no lies to spread about him, I got no complaints. He had lots of girls hangin' on him an' I pushed the other ones out, so he got the right to do what he cares to, an' I ain't in no position as it appears to make testimony against him....

PROSECUTOR: (*angrily*) Your Honor, my witness has obviously been intimidated—the court should know that her brother Conroy was found dead last night in—

KIDD: Objection! Your Honor, the prosecution is—

(SOUND: *gavel*)

PROSECUTOR: (*frustrated*) This is so obvious! (PROSECUTOR *sits.*)

BEATIE: What's obvious? Nothing is obvious!

KIDD: (*buoyant; approaching her happily*) Miss Roscoe, you have described Titus Skinner as your "boyfriend," have you not?

BEATIE: Yes. I mean ... I was with him for a while, but there were other girls ... like me ... other girls like me ... the same age ... an' ... an' ... (*laughs*) ... lookin' like me.

KIDD: And you are the sister of the murdered boy, Earl Roscoe, are you not?

BEATIE: That was his name. Yes. I think so, yes.

KIDD: How would you characterize your relationship with Mr. Skinner?

BEATIE: ... what was that word ... ? I, uh, I mixed-up. ...

KIDD: Was Titus ever violent toward you?

BEATIE: Oh no.

KIDD: Was he kind to you—bought you presents, bought your mother something for her birthday?

BEATIE: (*naively pleased*) Oh, you know about that? Yeah, Titus showed up with some crazy-big plant, some kind of complicated name to them, uh, with tinfoil an' a green ribbon wrapped around ... uh ... the flowers was dyed bright pink ... an' my Momma was still in bed an'. ... Jesus, she was so surprised! But how do you know about it ... ? (*shaking her head*) That Titus, he always done things to his own style!

KIDD: So the defendant was kind to you? Was he gentle to you, was he loving to you ... ?

BEATIE: Oh yes. Yes.

KIDD: Titus Skinner suffers from a bad reputation, would you say? a misleading reputation?

BEATIE: Oh Jesus yes. Yes. He just too big for the neighborhood an' the neighborhood tryin' to pull him down.

KIDD: The neighborhood, the people on the street, created a rumor to the effect that Titus Skinner and his friends were responsible for the murder of your brother and—

BEATIE: (*interrupting his last several words, as if not wanting to hear them*) Oh yeah! yeah! It was just nigger-talk... all kinds of jealous mother-fuckers, shootin' their damn mouths off.... On account of, you know, (*earnestly, to audience*) there is a low-lyin' mediocre element in the world, anxious to pull down big men... got to tear their wings off at the shoulders.... Now Titus, what he needed was, maybe, was, uh, he was like one of them famous generals only he was hid-away somewhere, like on a farm out in the country, feedin' the cows or whatever they got on a farm... and, uh, somebody come ridin' along on a horse an' told the news about a big invasion... an' the general, who was only a man feedin' cows at the time, why, he thrown all that shit down an' walked right out there an' walked right into the picture books.... Only, only Titus never got that kind of news brought to him: so he kind of, you know, kind of had to invent the way out for himself....

KIDD: Then in your intimate knowledge of Titus Skinner's character, Miss Roscoe, in your very intimate and yet objective assessment of the likelihood of his—of his being involved—in the crime of which he is accused, you would say—you would say—?

BEATIE: It's hands-off him. You better let him loose.

KIDD: You haven't been intimidated, Miss Roscoe, have you?

BEATIE: (*staring*)... huh?

KIDD: Recent, uh, developments... and the atmosphere of the case... haven't intimidated you, have they? You haven't been approached, I mean, by anyone, and threatened...? (*When* BEATIE *seems not to comprehend, he speaks simply and loudly, as if to a child.*) You haven't been coerced in any way, have you, Miss Roscoe?

BEATIE: (*after a long pause*) Coerced...? Coerced? (*The rest of the stage darkens again; the spotlight is on* BEATIE, *but mellow.*) Coerced...? What word is that...?

SCENE TWELVE

The courtroom.

TITUS: Howcome my attorney didn't want me to step up here, I don't know... he needs more faith in me... he's too nervous... I said to him *All them other people goin' to talk about me, an' I ain't goin' to be allowed up there?—ain't goin' to be allowed the final word?*

Jesus, that looked to me like a sure give-away, that I had something to hide, an' any jury at all, if they are all white people like this jury, or all black, or in-between, they are not goin' to take the correct impression out of that. My attorney said it was a strategy, his way, but I told him I determined the strategy of my own life. I always have done that, an' I always turned out O.K. . . . . Most of the time.

(TITUS *steps down from the witness stand, walks out onto the stage. He glances down at himself, checking his appearance, clears his throat, shows some signs of nervousness, but also eagerness, pleasure. It is obvious that he enjoys himself—his voice, his behavior, his being—and there is a kind of close, intimate awareness of his 'being,' which most of the other people in the play, especially Conroy and Mason and Beatie, do not exhibit; as if they were somehow strangers to themselves, trying to figure out what their relationship is to these strangers.* TITUS, *most of all, is not a 'healthy animal' but a healthy-seeming human being—the animalistic quality is important, he is physically impressive, strong, tall, etc., but it is subordinate to his more conscious awareness of himself. Yet he is not 'heroic'—he must be played as a murderer.*)

TITUS: A few years ago I had a dream . . . (*clearing his throat; louder*) A few years ago I had a dream . . . I mean a dream like at night . . . an' I don't have dreams like other people, almost never, I just fall into bed an' sleep hard, an' wake up all ready for the next day. But I had a dream, this dream (*indicates the scene around him*) that I was on trial . . . on trial for something I did or didn't do, or something somebody did, somewhere along the line . . . uh . . . an' damn if it don't all come back to me! I mean, I prophesized all this shit! —the talk, an' the way it looks here, people sittin' around gawkin' at me—rows an' rows of people starin' an' listenin'—damn if it wasn't a crazy dream, lookin' back on it, like you do with dreams that turn out to be true! . . . This dream come to me years ago, when I was just a skinny scrawny little kid, with no pride to me except what was layin' in wait, in my head. (*He touches his head, his face, as if presenting it to the audience; his manner is kingly, he considers himself worthy of display.*) I prophesized this scene for myself. It was Titus Skinner not yet thirty years old, on trial for murder in this city, in a courtroom that looked like this. Jesus, I had a real dream of it! And I woke up sweating and scared as hell an' I said to myself *Titus, better get the hell out of this city—you headin' for real trouble!* But, to keep a balance, I also said *Titus, there is risks necessary for any man.* So I hung around an' here I am today.... The dream had a judge, a white man like him, an', uh, lots of white people around...like the men askin' all the questions, one side an' then the other, my side an' then their side, all white men askin' questions an' presentin' a case, the way they do, according to their *strategy.* *(mockingly)* Which is the white man's strategy, like my attorney tried to say, keeping me from my own defense...it's courtroom strategy, so he told me, but hell with that. So this is the outcome of the dream: I in a bad spot, I sweatin' like a pig inside my new clothes, an' I really, uh, I really in for some trouble now, because they is all catchin' up with me an' tryin' to show how I did some crime, that is provable an' against the law. Jesus, how you like that?—that's a tight spot! So to get out of it I did some magic, real magic, like a trick of a magician, you know, that I never even thought about in real life, when I was awake, an' everything turned out O.K. That is the hell of it! The surprise of it!...One time my brother Mason, that is messed up now in the face an' in the head, an' who is right now layin' on the sofa in my Momma's living room, where he goin' to lay the rest of his life...my brother Mason, when he was a little kid, memorized a poem for school an' went around the house recitin' it, an' he got it down just perfect an' on the right day he went to school an' damn if he didn't say it out just perfect.... *(shakes his head)* Only time he ever done anything to impress me! The poem never made no sense to me, but it went along O.K. an' sounded O.K. Mason never done anything before or since that day. But anyway he done *that....* In my dream I perform a trick of magic, an' everybody so damn impressed they clap their hands an' say to the jail-people *Let Titus Skinner go free!* The people clap their hands though they hate me like hell, they *really* hate me, but, shit, they got to admit in their heads that I am high-level to bring off the trick, an' it in the fair play, you know, the interests of open market, that I got to be rewarded. *(looks around, gets silent assent)* So I will do that trick now an' see what happens....

(As if this isn't well-planned, he looks around and the court clerk, a servile white man, steps hesitantly forward, confers with TITUS *briefly, glances back at the* JUDGE, *hurries off-stage to reappear with a large light bulb and some wire, looped around his arm.* TITUS *gives him instructions, and while the clerk winds one end of*

the wire around TITUS's *ankle,* TITUS *wipes his forehead, turned
halfway to the audience. He is excited, keyed-up, nervous. The
clerk unwinds the wire until he is nearly out of sight in the darkness at the rear of the stage.)*

TITUS: You got that plugged in?—is there a socket back there? (*to
audience*) He pluggin' that in. All this is a wire for electricity, here.
See, it's got the insulation, or whatever they call it. And this-here is
a 100-watt bulb, it says so on the top of it . . . all this small part's too
trivial for my dream, the dream took care of itself an' didn't bother
with such nuisance. O.K., you got that plugged in? Now I will
explain: every black boy in America has a certain thought that he
grows up into, an' that is the electric chair . . . but damn if they
ain't gettin' rid of it, state by state . . . an' I expect it will turn up
like the wild animals in a museum somewhere, where you can't get
at it. That changes a way of life. That modifies a way of life. But I
was born at such a time that I had a long expectation of it, the
electric chair, an' it made me think fast, an' I come to like it, you
know, in a crazy way . . . how you get to like something you been
adjacent to for a while. . . . (*boastfully*) In fact, you people are
comin' to like *me* . . . I *very* adjacent to you. However, this is the
fact: that the trick of the electric-stuff is in my head, like in all
black boys' heads, an' their mommas naturally got that worry also,
so it a family enterprise. But I am not a nigger, I am something
else, an' that allow me to triumph over the shitty little trick of the
electric-magic, which is just some plugged-in strategy, that anybody could do if he pulled the switch. . . . So I take this 100-watt
bulb an' I display it like this (*holds it high, in his right hand; like
a sword or a torch*) an' I talk to myself in utter confidence . . . in the
magic, that it will work. You watch. (*He closes his eyes, holds one
hand to his forehead as if concentrating very hard.*) . . . Here is the
need for some hard concentration! (*He tries again, seems to be
straining, so that his face twists into a mask of anguish.*) This calls
for strong energies . . . all the flow-through of the energies that is
loose in here, an' in the universe . . . but I equal to it, I ain't goin'
to back away. . . .

(*Finally, the light bulb actually lights up.* TITUS *holds it proudly
aloft. He makes a slight, mocking bow to the audience and to the
people on stage with him, who applaud his trick falteringly—
some of them not clapping, only staring in horror; others clapping*

briskly but hollowly. TITUS *bows again to the real audience, as the stage lights dim slowly until only his light remains; then that is extinguished.)*

THE TRIUMPH OF THE
SPIDER MONKEY

The Triumph of the Spider Monkey was first performed in a Phoenix Playworks production, at The Playhouse Theatre, 359 W. 48 St., New York City, on December 19, 1979. The cast was as follows:

Bobbie Gotteson, The Spider Monkey .... Philip Casnoff

Judge, Danny Minx .... William Duell

Prosecutor, College Boy, Vlad J. .... Jonathan Hogan

Defense Attorney, Man, College Boy, Juror ...... James Rebhorn

Rosalind, Louise D., Doreen B. .... Alma Cuervo

Therapist, Melva .... Sylvia Miles

Directed by Daniel Freudenberger

NOTE:

The style of *The Triumph of the Spider Monkey* should be both ritual-istic and 'naturalistic.' Though the play's tone is frequently that of parodistic exuberance it is fundamentally imagined as a tragedy of a classic—that is, a sacrificial—sort.

It might be advisable to help the audience by way of titles (the Judge's announcements, etc.) shown on signs or with a slide projector.

CHARACTERS:

Bobbie Gotteson, late twenties

Judge

Prosecutor

Defense Attorney

Child Therapist

Melva McLaren

Danny Blecher aka Danny Minx

Vlad. J.

Rosalind

Louise

Doreen

Jurors, College Boys, Geoffrey, 'Victim,' Persons in Crowd

ACT ONE

PROLOGUE

Darkness. The chords of a guitar. A light slowly reveals BOBBIE
GOTTESON, *seated at the end of what will be the defense counsel's
table. He is a handsome young man, clean-shaven, flamboyantly
and naively dressed: with a red headband, a tight red shirt open to
show his chest, tight jeans, and high-heeled boots. He may also
wear a belt with an oversized buckle, chains around his neck, a
bracelet, etc. His manner is both eager and apprehensive; his smile
is sometimes intimidated, sometimes rather sinister. Throughout
the play* BOBBIE *tries to gauge others' response to him so that he
can 'know' who he is, or with what emotion he should respond
in turn.*

BOBBIE: (*in a slow threatening drawl*)

Slowly we are overrunning the earth
spidermonkeys twittering climbing leaping leering
on discount banjos

the Jukebox of the 40's could not cage us in
the 3-D cardboard viewer of the 50's
Cinemascope of the 60's
disco pulsebeat of the 70's

(*comes forward, addressing audience*)

Slowly we are overrunning the earth
spidermonkeys with long curly scruffy tails
spidermonkeys scuttling up drainpipes
spidermonkeys courting their brides

when the spidermonkeys Inside
open soul-doors to spidermonkeys Outside
the passion of Bobbie Gotteson
will be JUST ANOTHER HEADLINE—

SCENE ONE

A stylized court of law. JUDGE *banging gavel.*

JUDGE: Bailiffs!—gag that man! Tie him up and gag him! The Court
will not tolerate such behavior from a maniac on trial for his life—
Such monkeyshines—

BOBBIE: (*resisting; constrained*) You didn't let me finish my song!
There's more! All the stanzas are repeated—there's a powerful
coda at the end—

JUDGE: Counsel is advised to instruct his client to refrain from such
outbursts—such disgusting caterwauling— This is a Court of
Law, he is on trial for his life, we are *not* being televised—

BOBBIE: You didn't let me finish! If you let me finish you'd understand!
—you would be on my side—

DEFENSE ATTY.: (*in a high calm disdainful voice*) If it please Your
Honor and the Ladies and Gentlemen of the Jury (*He bows slightly
in their direction.*)—my client is now quieted down and there is
no need for physical restraints—though we should all feel more
comfortable— Bobbie—

BOBBIE: I want to take the stand! It's my turn! I don't want to wait!
Nosey crowds—always spectators—gawking at me—bastards—
You can't take photographs in here: it isn't allowed.

JUDGE: (*his announcement may be accompanied by a sign*) THE
NATIVITY OF THE MANIAC.

PROSECUTOR: It is a matter of public record, Your Honor, and Members of the Jury, that the Maniac Bobbie Gotteson was delivered to the world out of Locker 791-C of the Port Authority of New York—

FIRST WOMAN: I was just on my way to buy my ticket when I heard this funny little noise—a funny little *tinny* noise—like it was coming from far away—

PROSECUTOR: 10:38 PM. February 14, 1944. The Port Authority of New York City.

FIRST WOMAN: It wasn't any human sound but it was so pathetic—I couldn't just walk past—

MAN: Wailing and self-pity— shameless snivelling— I was trying to take a nap and suddenly there was this bawling—and what a stink!

(BOBBIE *shrinks in his chair, tries to hide his face.*)

SECOND WOMAN: What is this! What is this ugly noise!

MAN: Another mouth for us to feed. Taxes going up every day, no end in sight—

FIRST WOMAN: It's stopped crying.

MAN: It's still crying.

SECOND WOMAN: (*flailing shopping bag, angry*) Another baby in a foot-locker! You hear about them all the time!

MAN: It isn't a baby—not a human baby. Let me see—

SECOND WOMAN: Some of us don't dump our babies in foot-lockers in the Port Authority! Some of us show civilized restraint! We have pride—dignity—self-respect—respect for life—love and sympathy and Christian concern for others— We don't ask the tax-payers of this nation to finance our abortions—

PROSECUTOR: (*approaching* BOBBIE, *who tries to hide beneath table*) Now—now—now! Just what do we have here?

FIRST WOMAN: I saw her, I think—the mother. Tip-toeing away all innocent. Couldn't have been more than fifteen or sixteen years old— Filthy old sheepskin jacket, sneakers without socks—in this weather!—and sores on her mouth—

MAN: Naw, you're fulla shit. A big black gal, she was, jigglin' 'n' waddlin' all over, drunk, hair dyed red and frizzed to hell, walked right *past* me—

FIRST WOMAN: She had sores around her mouth—the pupils of her eyes were dilated—

SECOND WOMAN: They do it every day! You read about it every day! —Do you think sluts like that have the decency, the courtesy, the logic, to take advantage of abortion clinics located within easy bus-rides of their homes? No—they prefer to have their babies, and thumb their noses at us, and leave the disgusting soaked diapers for us to gag over—

FIRST WOMAN: Maybe it isn't even what we think, I didn't get a *good* look—

MAN: Hey, it ain't a baby after all—

SECOND WOMAN: Some of us love our children—we wouldn't dream of abandoning them in trash cans or incinerators or public lockers or orphanages—in vacant lots—in the oily harbor— What *is* it! What *is* that thing!

PROSECUTOR: (*pulls* BOBBIE *out, stands him up*) Come on out, you little monkey! C'mon, c'mon, c'mon out you furry little monkey!

SECOND WOMAN: Blessed Mary! It *is* a monkey!

MAN: It's still alive—

FIRST WOMAN: The cutest little monkey, but my goodness!—he needs his diaper changed!

PROSECUTOR: C'mon you monkey-ugly little bastard! Kitchee-kitchee-kitchee-koo! Don't you pull any tricks!

SECOND WOMAN: Hispanic blood—you can see it—

BOBBIE: (*pulling away, cringing, appealing to audience*) A uniform— hands— Grabbing me— I wasn't ready—

MAN: That ain't no human baby, my friends—it's a jigaboo! .

BOBBIE: Out of the darkness and delivering me to light— But he was so rough—

FIRST WOMAN: Oh it is cute! Just the darlingest thing! And it's *white!*

BOBBIE: (*coming forward as the others fall back*) Stuffed in a duffel bag for eight hours! Hungry and bawling! I wasn't in full possession of my wits—you must understand. I gave away my rights—my constitutional rights—too cheaply! I surrendered everything too cheaply! (*in a confidential voice*) If I signed any confession it was under duress. We all know that. They worked me over in the precinct house and wouldn't let me sleep.

JUDGE: Restrain that man! You all know perfectly well that this is a Court of Law—authorized by the great Commonwealth of California to administer justice—it is *not* Amateur Night once again at the boys' reformatory.

BOBBIE: I'm not an amateur! I'm a professional! I had a real job at Lucky Pierre's even if they don't say so, now—I auditioned for it like anyone else and got it—slept on the beach the night before and my voice was a little husky but I got the job anyway. I was a real professional before Melva and her friends came along, I can prove it—(*seizing guitar, attempting to sing*) I declare this trial adjourned! I declare the jury hung! The judge unseated! The attorneys disbarred! (*the guitar is taken from him*) Look: I didn't give you any authority to bring me to life—to slap me on the back and set me going. Who called the ambulance? Where was I taken? If I signed papers I don't remember—I was coerced! I didn't even have a name! Nobody ever named me! I refuse to answer to the name "Bobbie Gotteson" which is a made-up mocking name! I wasn't there, I'm innocent— I don't know whose blood it was— (BOBBIE *quiets and returns to his seat.*)

PROSECUTOR: Your Honor—Ladies and Gentlemen of the Jury— Ladies and Gentlemen of the Courtroom—I submit to you as evidence: you have just witnessed the delivery of the screaming red-faced monkey-ugly diaper-soaked Bobbie Gotteson, parentage unknown, out of locker 791-C of the great Port Authority of New York. Yes, you may very well shrink back in revulsion. An illegitimate baby, an illegal baby, the maniac Bobbie Gotteson already berserk and in trouble with the law—

DEFENSE ATTY.: (*rising*) Now I really should object—I think I really *should*—

PROSECUTOR: —already set upon a career of anti-social acts that, gaining sickening momentum this past year, will culminate in the most widely publicized of recent mass-murders on the Coast—

DEFENSE ATTY.: Your Honor, isn't he prejudicing the jury?

PROSECUTOR: I have the facts! The most exquisite, repulsive details, many of them hitherto withheld from the media! And—here—the murder weapon itself— (*The Machete is briefly displayed as if teasingly. All are interested with the exception of* BOBBIE, *who covers his eyes.*) And it is my point, Your Honor, that the maniac's career of crime was ordained *from the very first*. What else can emerge from a urine-stinking locker except our Bobbie Gotteson— in the flesh! His chromosomes were badly askew—

BOBBIE: I challenge that! I'll leave my brain to the Neuropsychiatric Department of the Medical Institute of Los Angeles—they've been begging me!—and we'll see. We'll see about that libel!

DEFENSE ATTY.: (*reluctantly, disdainfully*) Your Honor, this *does* strike me as grossly unfair. Everyone is being prejudiced. Even if the Prosecution has all the facts on hand, and is essentially correct... what about fair play?... aren't there courtroom rules to be observed? (*spitefully*) Even if I did accept this repulsive case for the challenge of it! For *no fee!* (It's completely false that I have already sold book and film rights for my memoirs—you'll find my signature on no contract.) I didn't come here this morning to be made a fool of by Mack—I mean the Prosecution— (*pacing about*) Yes, you may quote me! It was simply out of idealism that I accepted the Gotteson case! "The most appealing of recent mass murderers in the State of California"—as the tabloid press has tagged him. But from the very first this trial has been unfair—the jurors have been prejudiced by my client's appearance—his intolerable music —his very *existence*. Imagine, a defendant who is not only guilty but insane as well: as his pathetic bragging about a job at Lucky Pierre's, and having made a pilot film attest—and an intimate friendship with Melva McLaren who denies all knowledge of him— It's too absurd, it's too degrading for an attorney of my stature—

(*Lights dim; focus on* BOBBIE.)

BOBBIE: (*pleading*) He wasn't there, he doesn't know! ...The diapers were changed. They cleaned me up. Gave me shots. Wormed me. Then the joking started.... (BOBBIE *walks in a circle, restrained by shadowy figures he tries not to acknowledge.*) Hospital!—orphanage!—foster homes: one two three four *five*. Boys' Reformatory.

Boys' Reformatory again. Then State Prison. And now—a fucking little cell without even a cellmate to keep me warm! Seventeen years four months fourteen days spent Inside. And the years spent Outside—I almost can't remember. (*smooths hair, straightens shoulders, smiles*) But—! I was always one for jokes! Making light of things! Joking got the little monkey in trouble sometimes but what the hell! A cheerful manner—basic optimism—a basic American optimism that sank upon occasion, or was stomped flat, but always surfaced again: *Things work out for the best, in the end! You can't keep the kid down! He* mocked Amateur Night but he wasn't there—he didn't hear the applause and the whistling and the yodelling— (*high-pitched voice*) Oh Bobbie come back on stage! Oh Bobbie Bobbie Bobbie! Give us Bobbie! (*pause*) Sometimes they begged the little monkey to stop, they laughed so hard. Popular opinion divided about equally between the *spider-monkey-climbing-up-a-greased-pole* routine (*mimes this*) and the *spastic-crossing-the-freeway* routine. (*He mimes this, his 'audience' is greatly amused.*) There was also *huge-fish-fighting-hook-in-mouth* which involved squirming and writhing on the floor...and my arms had to be taped to my sides...and my ankles taped together ...a lot of work...and it always hurt me...no matter how hard they laughed...or applauded...it always hurt me. (*pause*) *But* I had a natural talent even as a boy for show business, for pleasing the crowd. Even in therapy sessions I convulsed them. *Oh Bobbie don't stop! Bobbie Bobbie Bobbie!* Melva used to wipe tears from her cheeks—

VOICE: (*contemptuously*) Melva McLaren denies any knowledge of you! We all deny any knowledge of you!

SCENE TWO

Lights up. JUDGE *announces:* THE MANIAC EXPLAINS HIS SANITY TO THE COURT.

BOBBIE: (*disingenuously*) All right, look: I can play sane like you. Like everyone. Sometimes I played insane...that's true...but now I am very sane. It's a matter of *concentration.* (*pause*) Lots of times my life was saved by playing insane. The first time, in jail in Denver where I was picked up for vagrancy, I woke up to find a man—a complete stranger—a wire-bearded drooling bastard staring into

my face. (BOBBIE *mimes the scene.*) *My little girl!* he was mewing.
My little girl—where have you been for so long? He tried to embrace me—tried to kiss me. I started fighting, but he was heavier
than me, and kept saying *My little girl, my little girl,* and put his
hand over my mouth, and I went wild, I was terrified of suffocating, I managed to get him off me and started hitting him—hard
—while all these other fuckers stood around giggling—I butted
him in the face with my head—*Like hell Bobbie Gotteson is your
little girl!* . . . I must have blacked out because when I came to I was
still kicking him and his face was pretty well smashed and the
other men in the cell were yelling for help like they were afraid
of *me* . . . and . . . and so . . . I proceeded to go crazy. It saved me from
a beating by the sheriff's men.

(BOBBIE *calms himself; wipes his face with a red handkerchief.*)

Well—from there I was transferred to a psychiatric hospital in the
mountains. It was one of those places where you got tokens for
behaving right, instead of being hosed down and beaten, so since I
was always a superb actor I acted chagrined and reformed . . . and
eventually accumulated most of the tokens in the hospital. Yes,
clever Bobbie could barely walk, his pockets were so heavy with
tokens! After a while the vagrancy charges were dropped, or whatever they were, maybe the papers got lost, so I was released . . . I had
a wonderful dark tan by then, and the pimples on my back had
cleared up. This was helpful in the next phase of my career.

(BOBBIE *mimes the next sequence, with* GEOFFREY *and the* VICTIM. *A
stuffed falcon, two helmets, and two leather whips are used.*)

Another time, out here on the Coast, my life was saved the same
way . . . about ten miles north of here. Lucky Pierre put me in contact with a guy named Geoffrey who was a part-time actor . . . and
one night he came to pick me up at the Club . . . but he told me to
leave my guitar behind, it wouldn't be needed tonight. Well—hell!
I was disappointed! I was *hurt!* I asked if the client had changed
his mind, if the party was called off, and Geoffrey said well, no, the
client has not changed his mind exactly but the instructions had
been altered. He said—begin by putting on this blindfold. So I
did. I couldn't refuse despite my high principles because I had no
money at all right then—*no money at all.* And I was far, far from
the only person who had ever loved me purely, for myself, I had

lost Danny Minx forever, and so...and so I hadn't any choice. I put on the blindfold and pretended I couldn't see. (Though actually I could see around the edges.) But I had enough sense not to leave the guitar behind, because the guitar was priceless, it was my own soul, and if something happened to it.... Well, you'll soon see what the consequences were, when something happened to Gotteson's guitar! ...So Geoffrey drove up into the Hills, and I tried to relax, and we stopped somewhere out in the country, and Geoffrey said O.K., I guess you can take the blindfold off now, it's already past ten and the old guy was adamant about us being there on the dot at ten, and not a minute later. So we got out of the car and Geoffrey opened the trunk and took out two leather whips with little fringes or whatever-you-call-them, and a leather wrist-band with the queerest damn thing stuck to it....

(BOBBIE *is outfitted.*)

...I asked him what the hell that was, it had eyes that really penetrated into your soul, more piercing even than my own, I think!... but Geoffrey was getting anxious about the time, and had dropped the slip of paper with the address somewhere in the dark, and couldn't find it, and he said shut up and buckle it on and let's get going, I got the address memorized, it's right across the street, and he put a helmet on me with a feathery plume, and another for himself.... And as we tromped through the brush he explained the assignment to me. We would be told to stop our assault, he said, but we must not stop, we must not even hesitate, and if the client screamed *Mercy!* our instructions were to shout *No mercy! No mercy!* —and continue beating the client as ordered. Now this *was* a change from the evening of music and trying-out-of-new-almost-completed songs I had anticipated, but I began at once to concentrate all my powers inside my head, so that I could feel the energy accumulating...and by the time we smashed our way through a terrace door and into the living room where a man sat in a bathrobe watching the weather report, I was all aflame...all aflame...and could not have been stopped even by bullets. The falcon too had come alive. I could feel it quivering, ready for the attack. The client, seeing my face, began to scream. We rushed in and used our whips and there was no stopping me—there was no mercy! (*pause*) Now—you'll want to take special notes on this— What happened was: I danced and lunged and went wild, I was galvanized by energy, and joined, *for split seconds at a time,* by invisible helpers, whose identity I couldn't, at the time, determine. That was the first known instance of that phenomenon. I was using the whip, and the falcon, and showing no mercy!...But then I was being dragged somewhere, Geoffrey was shouting at me, it was a mistake, we had broken into the wrong house, the client was waiting next-door, I must stop what I was doing, Geoffrey had hold of my hair and was trying to drag me away, and I screamed *No mercy! No mercy!* and turned upon Geoffrey with the whip and the falcon. What did he mean, Gotteson must stop? *Gotteson* must stop? On the contrary, Gotteson need never stop. Once begun, Gotteson is unstoppable. Inertia! Momentum! The secret of the universe! Energy! Dance! Spirit! Flow! *No mercy!* (*pause*) But then, a few minutes later, I saw...I saw what...I saw what I had done...and...and...(*pause*) And though I was remarkably cool, remarkably sane, I saw that only madness would save me: so I shifted my spirit into that realm and blanked out while winding the whip about Geoffrey's throat, so that whatever happened—and I aimed for strangling him into unconsciousness, not into death—would not be, strictly speaking, within the province of my responsibility. And I don't, to this day, know exactly what *did* happen.... Is Geoffrey here? (*peering out*) I work up to brilliant sunshine, two hundred miles up the coast in Monterey.... (*pause*) A maniac is immortal.... He cannot be killed, except by his own mind-directives.

(BOBBIE, *with his guitar, strolls to the other side of the stage, to the courtroom area, which is now illuminated.* JUDGE, ATTORNEYS, JURORS, *etc. He strums and sings.*)

The Courtship of the Spider Monkey

There she is awaiting him
alone in a hole
that is a room
in a house honeycombed
with holes

hand-over-hand he climbs
foot-over-foot up the side of the house
the master of gravity!
concentrated and tremulous as a bridegroom!

the Moon and the Machete
communicate in lewd winks

(*The* MACHETE *is unveiled by the* PROSECUTOR; *it has been hidden by a scarlet cloth. There is a stir in the courtroom: one of the jurors, a plump, well-dressed man of youngish middle age, with glasses, rises to get a better look.*)

BOBBIE: (*strumming suggestively, with a leer*)

the Moon and the Machete
communicate in lewd winks!

The Machete was three feet long, a gift from Vlad J., for use in one of our films. A blade of steel—a handle you could get a grip on! *That* machete isn't it. You can't see the Machete except by moonlight. (*haltingly*) Doreen waited...like a space...to be threaded, the way you thread a needle. I...I...had nothing against her. She brought me home with her. I.... The moment has been obscured! There's been so much in the newspapers.... (*pause*) I didn't fall in love with her! I was never that weak.

SCENE THREE

Lights up. JUDGE *announces:* SOCIAL WELFARE AND FAMILY SERVICES AGENCY, MILLSTONE COUNTY, NEW JERSEY —WINTER MORNING 1960. *The* THERAPIST *and* BOBBIE (*as a young boy*) *face each other across the table. The* THERAPIST's *manner is brisk, professional, and uninflected. (The role may be played by either a man or a woman.)* BOBBIE *is frightened but, at times, defiant and bold.*

THERAPIST: Your mother...your foster mother...is in the hospital? And from her hospital bed has issued another complaint? (*shuffling through papers*) She actually had to call the police on you and your brothers, did she!

BOBBIE: ...not my brothers. I don't have any brothers.

THERAPIST: Your foster father, I have a memo here, ah yes, your foster father has told authorities he can no longer handle you or the other boys; he's giving up. (*peering at note*) *I am at the end of my rope,* he says. Six misspellings in eight words....

BOBBIE: They did things to me. Buck, he's sixteen, he weighs 190 pounds....

THERAPIST: Ah here, your files: ah yes: a score of -43 on the Wenshler Verbal Skills test at the age of 3...Hardison-Radt Abstraction-Perception in the 79th percentile...Pyne-Manatee Conceptualizing Abilities verging on the frankly pathological.... And the fine print: faulty liaison between right and left brain hemispheres... disjointed motor coordination...latent psychosis, left frontal lobe ...(*looks up, peering at* BOBBIE *who is touching his head gingerly*) ...scaly flaking skin...constant humming and singing under breath. On the Witherspoon Block Skills test, it says here, you rammed the square blocks into the triangular holes, *rammed* them until wood chips flew and the set was destroyed and you had to be carried away. —Eh? What's that? Are you sniffling?

BOBBIE: Buck did things to me. With all the kids watching. He tied my wrists to the furnace door-handle—it was hot there—

THERAPIST: And here is a sheath of poems...with a ribbon around them!...poems written, it is notated, at the age of ten. About which your teacher at Rahway Junior High has said in this memo: *The product of a diseased mind.* (*reads disdainfully*)

The Train

a toy train the size of a real train
was stalled in a dark winter field

BOBBIE: (*snatching poem away*)

a toy train the size of a real train
was stalled in a dark winter field
the temperature on both sides of the windows was 0°
the passengers were shouting to me for help
the ax flew across the New Jersey plains
when it returned home it was bloody
there were hairs on it

I hid it beneath my pillow
where nobody ever found it

THERAPIST: Ridiculous!—not a rhyme in it. You'll never be a poet.

BOBBIE: Buck tied my wrists real tight, he didn't need to tie them so tight.... They said afterward I bit his lip and wouldn't let go... they had to pry my jaws open....

THERAPIST: Ah I see, I had the wrong memo earlier: it's your mother who is at the end of her rope. And your father—ah, your father is deceased. Why didn't you say so at once, my boy! You and your foster brothers will all be moved immediately. The law requires that you have two parents—both living—a *mother* and a *father*.

BOBBIE: It wasn't my father. God is my father.

THERAPIST: Are you still sniffling? It's obvious that you need love, even a creature like you, but who has the stomach for it? I was made for better things...more refined, philosophical issues...the great questions of good and evil, for instance...subtleties...not crude case histories like *you*.

BOBBIE: They laughed at me. They shouldn't have laughed at me. God was watching....

THERAPIST: (*briskly*) Well—I'm afraid we'll have to shift you all about once more! Musical chairs! The law's the law!

BOBBIE: I'm ready to go.

THERAPIST: Ah: there's a notation here to the effect that we *might* just transfer you to Boys' Reformatory directly. Save a few steps. Well ...I don't know.... *How* many stitches did your poor brother require in his lip...? (*peering at papers, drops some*)

BOBBIE: I'm ready to go. I don't sleep. Night or day. You can't take that chance—sleeping. I'm ready. I'm awake.

THERAPIST: That's fascinating. And you're—how old?—eleven? You look a great deal older than eleven to *me*. (*studies him*) In fact you're about the hairiest eleven-year-old to come through this office in years.

(BOBBIE *touches his face, rubs his neck self-consciously.*)

THERAPIST: You...shave? Don't you? At the age of eleven?

BOBBIE: I don't shave. I don't know how.

THERAPIST: My boy, when I was in my twenties I was so idealistic!...I read Simone Weil, for instance . . . on the subject of self-effacement and saintliness. The need to, you know, eradicate one's ego . . . embrace lepers if that was necessary . . . though there are very few lepers today: they seem to have concentrated upon Africa. But idealism has its limits. I reached them quite quickly. Six months out of graduate school. . . . *Do* you shave? At the age of eleven?

BOBBIE: I'm ready to go. They threw my things in a box — it's on the back porch — but I don't even need it. Please don't hit me. It wasn't my fault they had to pry my jaws open with a screwdriver.

THERAPIST: (*repressing shudder*) Another foster home, or the orphanage, or Boys' Reformatory — it hardly makes any difference. Boys like you don't appreciate what the County does for you. You stay out of school, turn viciously upon your families or your teachers, gather in tides of venereal disease to swamp the continent, coast to coast. An *epidemic* of you. (*rises, stacks papers together, turns to address the audience*) It was no secret to me that Bobbie Gotteson would be involved in murder, and worse, within a few years. From the looks of those shoulder and arm muscles . . . that hard little torso . . . the psychopathic glint in the eyes. *But* — ! The poor boy won't make a penny out of it! All the money will go to other people, including the former movie star Melva McLaren whose memoirs will be *rather* scorching. And the leading role in the film will go to a much taller, more handsome actor. (*to* BOBBIE, *pityingly*) You're just too ugly to be taken seriously, even with a machete in hand. Are you crying? But why? I'll compromise and transfer you directly into Children's Detention, that way we'll get you off the streets, your foster brothers are there already, waiting for you. So you needn't snivel about loneliness. Bobbie Gotteson; or Gadsen; or Gotsen; whatever this word is. . . . Are you crying?

BOBBIE: I don't cry.

SCENE FOUR

Lights up. JUDGE *announces:* HOW THE MANIAC BOBBIE GOTTESON TRAVELLED TO THE COAST. DANNY BLECHER *also known as* DANNY MINX *steps forward to address audience in a hoarse, nervous, jocular voice. He clears his throat frequently, fusses with his cuffs. He is in his mid- or late forties, his graying hair recedes sharply from his temples, his skin is pasty-white, and his jaw is stubbled with beard. He wears a cheap but 'stylish' sports coat, possibly in a plaid or a check design; his shirt is open at the throat; he is tieless. His trousers are stained and badly wrinkled.*

DANNY: It was me—it was *I*—Danny Minx—who was Bobbie Gotteson's Old Man at Rahway Correctional 'way back then. Nobody believes me now! Guys I hang around with these days don't believe me. 'Course it was a long time ago...I was younger then, and all muscle...Bobbie was just a kid...his future was all before him. So even if he knew my whereabouts and the Court could subpoena me he prob'ly wouldn't invite me to participate as a character witness...I guess I sort of let the kid down. Though I would be pleased and proud to testify in his behalf. (*gestures toward* BOBBIE) I was his first Old Man and never meant to break his heart. Things just happen. We had a misunderstanding in Wyoming or Colorado or one of them states. But I *always* had a fond memory of him... the way I taught him certain skills and techniques and methodologies in Rahway. (*fondly*) He was such a terrified little baby when they threw him in somebody *had* to step forward to protect him.

(BOBBIE *steps forward, cringing.* DANNY'S *tone is convivial but threatening. He caresses Bobbie, speaking in a strident hypnotic manner.*)

DANNY: Baby Bobbie Gotteson. What'd they get you for?

(BOBBIE *whispers.*)

DANNY: What!

(BOBBIE *stares at floor, embarrassed.*)

DANNY: You *what*—? Was the teacher a man or a woman?

(BOBBIE *stands silent.*)

DANNY: D'ya have witnesses? —I s'pose it was right in class! Right in front of the class! Yeh? How many years did you get?

(BOBBIE *makes a furtive gesture, signaling two or three fingers.*)

DANNY: She didn't die, then—? *Was* it a woman?

(BOBBIE *nods faintly*.)

DANNY: You hated her, eh? Did you? Real bad, eh? She picked on you in class, did she? (*fondly*) You don't look like a kid that's going to tolerate that kind of shit from anyone. —You hated her, did you?

(BOBBIE *shrugs his shoulders; looks frightened*.)

DANNY: Sure you did. You hated her. Baby Bobbie Gotteson—you'll get over that babyfaced look! (*caressing him*) The first lesson, my boy, is hate. I don't mean lazy sloppy weak effeminate hate but powerful concentrated wild manly *Hate*. Directed toward all our enemies. Yours and mine. And women—

BOBBIE: Women? Where?

DANNY: Hate hate hate hate hate. C'mon! (*squeezing his neck*) *Hate hate hate hate hate.*

BOBBIE: (*weakly*) Hate...hate....

DANNY: *Hate hate hate hate hate.*

BOBBIE: (*mumbling*) Hate hate hate...hate...hate hate hate *hate*....

DANNY: You even think about women, my boy, I'll twist off your balls! How's that?

BOBBIE: *Hate hate hate hate...hate HATE*....

DANNY: Louder! With strength and precision! Like Danny. *HATE.*

BOBBIE: HATE HATE HATE HATE....

DANNY: That's better! ...It's been good for us, hasn't it, Bobbie? From our first acquaintançe onward...we knew our destiny...you *know* about such things. (*to audience*) Well—the months flew by! Years flew by! It's all the same year inside and anyway me and Bobbie scorned to take note of the calendar. He was so sweet then —most days—a tame little monkey Danny Minx could command to do tricks. And talented too. Oh yes! (*to* BOBBIE) Now Bobbie, my plan is: you stay right here in the city, get a job right here, save money, and wait for me. I'll be out on parole in seven months. You wait for me, my boy, and never direct your thoughts anywhere else...for as you know (*squeezing him hard*) I have the ability to read your mind. I can see right into your mind. (*pause*) I have the ability, too, to leave my body at will ... to roam the streets freely ... eat food off the plates of diners in fancy restaurants ... have all the liquor I want ... do whatever I wish ... and to return to my physical shape by wake-up. Isn't that correct?

BOBBIE: Oh yes, Danny. Yes. You said you'd teach me the rest of the powers....

DANNY: But those powers, in immature hands, are dangerous! (*laughing*) D'you think that *you*, Baby Bobbie Gotteson, could manage such white-hot lethal powers of the mind? With your latent schizophrenic tendencies? With your charming but (*pinches his cheek*) *erratic* personality?

BOBBIE: You said you'd teach me the secret powers ... in front of witnesses you promised ... and now I have to leave you ... and what if you don't get out in seven months....

DANNY: Don't you give me no sass! Seven months is nothing in our lives, a mere snap of the fingers!

BOBBIE: But I'll be all alone.... I don't know how to be all alone....

DANNY: I'll be there, beside you. In your thoughts. Have faith. And don't fool around. *You know what I mean.* Eh? As soon as I look upon your face, my boy, when we meet again, I'll know whether you've been true to your Danny ... I'll know what action to take.

BOBBIE: I don't want to leave! I don't know how to get through the day without you!

DANNY: (*obviously gratified*) Bobbie, the real world beckons. The real world is awaiting. Get a job, don't violate even the smallest laws, think of me constantly, and pursue your musical career. That is Danny's wish, my boy: *Pursue your musical career.*

BOBBIE: Pursue my musical career....

DANNY: And soon I will be joining you. And we will make a life together, your musical genius and my genius for organization and financial manipulation. We will flee to the West Coast where a man has a chance....

BOBBIE: Those bastards that laughed at me, on Amateur Night ... they said, they said.... (*suddenly furious*) They said I was without a shred of talent! They hooted, they jeered, they pulled off their smelly shoes and threw them at me! I want them dead!

DANNY: (*mildly alarmed*) The best strategy, Bobbie, which all artists have known, is to perfect your art. Perfect your art, and leave ignorant fools gaping. Your genius will be your revenge....

BOBBIE: You *will* teach me the higher levels of the mind...?

DANNY: Perfect your art, my boy. And make us both millionaires.

BOBBIE: You have faith in me? In my talent? (DANNY *embraces him wordlessly.*)

(BOBBIE *advances, wiping tears from his eyes. At first he is too moved to speak. His speech is slow and broken, and then gains momentum.* BOBBIE *should always give the impression of being only precariously in control of himself.*)

BOBBIE: So I loaded and unloaded trucks in Rahway, for Allied Vans, and took guitar and singing lessons from José Fernandez who owned a music store downtown; he said he was from Spain but I think he was from the Bronx; a little nervous guy, always worried the store was going to shut down. The price of my lessons was six dollars a week but I believe it was worth every penny. In all things my Old Man directed me. There was *never a moment* night or day when I didn't have him beside me. Pursue your musical career, Danny whispered, have faith in your genius, make us both millionaires.... So it came about that songs poured into me. I would start humming, and melodies came out of the air, forcing themselves into me almost with violence. I could even 'receive' words if I hit upon the correct tunes. (*picks up his guitar, which he hugs; then begins to strum lightly*) Mr. Fernandez had me play the guitar for people browsing in the store, Saturday afternoons, like one of those wandering minstrels, and I picked around and played the songs I was practicing for him but then...somehow...I don't know how...maybe it was Danny's spirit...Danny whispering secret love-words in my ear...somehow my fingers just started playing, all by themselves, and I knew the words to songs, I could sing them right out of the air, in a wonderful strong vibrant lyric voice—

O you're eatable
non-repeatable!

O you're eatable
non-repeatable!

O you're eatable
non-repeatable!

and a number of people, mainly kids, but one distinguished-
looking silvery-haired gentleman, asked for my autograph; and
there were invitations to parties, to Hawaii, to somebody's pent-
house in Elizabeth for a private recording session, lots of women
milling around, women of all ages, offering to mend my jacket
(where the elbows were out), fatten me up with vitamins, that kind
of transparent thing, but I explained to them all—my old man
Danny would kill me. If I fucked around. So I *did* remain faithful
to him, and I *did* perfect my musical talent in those terrible lonely
wintry seven months we were apart. (*strums guitar, in a moody
melancholy way*) After all—what gives meaning to life but *love?*
It's why (*with dramatic strums of the guitar*)—we—are—all—on
—earth. (*with a harsh laugh*) And then—everything changed!

(DANNY *and* TWO COLLEGE BOYS *appear. Simulation of automobile
ride.* DANNY *is in the driver's seat, peers frequently into the rear-
view mirror or turns around to look at his passengers. He is in
high spirits, cavalier and a bit audacious, but during this scene it is
not clear whether his interest in the boys is genuine, or a ploy to
bait* BOBBIE. *But his alarm at* BOBBIE'*s final violence is genuine.*)

BOBBIE: (*to audience, as he joins* DANNY *and the* BOYS, *mid-stage*) Oh I
waited for him and I was faithful to him, just like the words of a
song, and when he got out I stole a car and we drove West. The
hell, he said, with his parole, nobody could catch *him* once he got
going, once his mind-powers were consolidated, so I stole a late-
model Buick, eight cylinders, and it *was* a honeymoon for a while,
just me and Danny Minx, my Old Man, and he called me Baby
Bobbie which always meant he was in a good mood and then—
and then just the other side of Wichita the trouble began—

DANNY: Hitch-hikers! In that hot sun! Poor boys! And we have so much
room in this marvelous car!

BOBBIE: Wait—what are you doing— We don't want anybody else—

DANNY: (*as* BOYS *climb in back seat*) Welcome, welcome! Welcome! How far west are you bound, my friends?

(*Though the* BOYS *are evidently college boys, wearing T-shirts with university names or logos, they mumble inarticulately, rather like morons. Their manner alternates between boldness and fear, and by the end of the scene they are clearly terrified.*)

DANNY: Now isn't that a coincidence! So are we. The lovely sandy beaches of Southern California. *Isn't* that a coincidence! Is the wind too much for you? Should I roll the window up? Bobbie— roll *your* window up, there's too much breeze. No? It's all right? Well—just let me know. I wouldn't want either of you to be discomforted in my car.

BOBBIE: (*muttering*) You ain't going to bring them along to California with us, are you—? Danny—?

DANNY: Come a far distance? Eh?

(BOYS *mumble and giggle, exchanging glances.*)

DANNY: East Coast college? Yeh? My God, Yale—what a coincidence! Glad to meet you, boys (*reaching hand around*)—Class of '53, myself— God, Bobbie (*winking, leering*) what a coincidence!

(*The* BOYS *hesitate, but shake his hand. Again they exchange glances, suppressing startled laughter.*)

DANNY: Now don't tell me you went to *Exeter* too? No? Well—that would be *too* much of a coincidence. And what do you major in at Yale, let me guess—Classics? No? Not Classics?

BOBBIE: (*restless, agitated, beginning to lose control*) Danny, I think you better stop this car. Danny, I think you better let them out.

DANNY: Would you boys like a little liquid refreshment? Bobbie, reach into the glove compartment there—that's a good boy— (BOBBIE *sullenly complies. The bottle is passed to the* BOYS, *who then offer Danny and Bobbie a cigarette.*) Thanks but I think not—though it's *very* thoughtful of you—I belong to the alcoholic era—I never imbibe drugs—though my rambunctious little friend here has tried nearly everything, haven't you, Bobbie? They say—but perhaps it is false?—that marijuana affects potency. *Is* it false? Yes?

Are there any reliable methods for determining that fact?

(*The* BOYS *pass the bottle back and forth, clearly not wanting to drink from it. But since* BOBBIE *is watching, they feel obliged — pretending to drink, and surreptitiously wiping the mouth of the bottle.*)

BOBBIE: What the hell are you doing! Ain't that shit good enough for you!

DANNY: (*patting* BOBBIE'*s knee*) Now, now, Bobbie, what kind of a way is that to talk to two guests? They been out in the hot sun despairing of *ever* getting a ride, and along we come, Danny and Baby Bobbie, and suddenly the cosmos is benign, and it *is* benign, and why do you want to spoil everything? (*twisting* BOBBIE'*s wrist*) Eh?

BOBBIE: (*agitated*) What are you saying, what kind of talk is that, I don't understand that kind of talk, you better stop this car and let these two out before something happens!

DANNY: (*glancing back at the* BOYS) I hear tell the *strangest* things these days, maybe you can inform a puzzled old alum: Yale is now co-ed and even the residence halls are co-ed and *what*, my dears, *what precisely does that mean?* It's indeed mouthwatering but I somehow cannot grasp—

BOBBIE: (*snatching back the bottle, taking a swig*) You don't want to hear about any old nasty co-ed places, Danny, whyn't you have me sing for you, I got the wildest idea for a song just a few miles back — Danny —

DANNY: (*as the* BOYS *mumble and gesticulate and break into nervous laughter*) JESUS GOD, is that so! Well I never—! *Is* that so! And I bet you two get your fair share, don't you, and more?—don't you? —eh?—with those big eyes and curly hair—

(BOBBIE *smashes the bottle on the dashboard. Turns to face the* BOYS.)

BOBBIE: You better get the hell out of here. Now. Open the doors. Now. *Now.*

DANNY: Now Bobbie what on earth—! Bobbie— He's just joking, boys, he's *such* a card—

BOBBIE: (*yelling, slashing at the* BOYS, *who cower away*) Your time is up! This is it! Death on the Great Plains! Bobbie Gotteson will not be trifled with!

DANNY: (*alarmed*) Bobbie! Stop! We'll have an accident— Wait— Let me pull over to the side—

BOBBIE: Grinning and smirking at us! Aren't you! Giggling behind your hands! Think you're too good for us, don't you! College boys —scared shitless—momma's boys—well momma ain't anywhere near to save you now—

(DANNY *grabs hold of* BOBBIE *and wrestles him back. The bottle falls. The stage darkens until only* BOBBIE *and* DANNY *remain illuminated.* BOBBIE *is sobbing as* DANNY *holds him, pats and strokes him, rocks him slightly, like a baby.*)

DANNY: (*murmuring*) Now, now, Bobbie, now, now, you're all right, you're absolutely fine, how does it go—you're eatable, non-repeatable, oh you're eatable, non-repeatable— (*Long pause.* BOBBIE *continues to sob,* DANNY *wipes his face.*) You shouldn't have hurt those boys, Bobbie. Those were innocent boys.

BOBBIE: (*vaguely*) I didn't—hurt—any boys. I didn't—hurt—

DANNY: Don't you remember?

BOBBIE: There's nobody here—nobody can come between us—

DANNY: (*sharply*) Don't you remember?

(BOBBIE *drifts off to sleep, curled on the car seat, and* DANNY *carefully extricates himself and sits staring at* BOBBIE *for a while. The scene darkens slowly.*)

BOBBIE: (*steps forward into light; fully awake; angry*) That song—you heard it—"Eatable"—was stolen from me by a two-bit composer at Vanbrugh Studios. It was used as the maudlin background music for one of their shitty beach movies! They stole my life's-work and changed the tempo of my songs, and the lyrics, and the titles, and had me evicted and arrested and thrown into a hole like a monkey!—like a monkey in a zoo! Treated me like an animal! Refused me my dignity as a human being! Wouldn't let me stand upright like a man! (*pause*) And all because of...all because of Danny Minx abandoning me. (*pause*) The thing I couldn't imagine happened: Danny abandoned me. In Colorado. In the hot pitiless sun. Abandoned me. (*pause*) And my life's-work forever afterward doomed to be stolen and·mangled and fouled by ignorant hands! (*pause*) The next day... after the college boys... and I didn't touch a hair on their heads, I *know* I didn't!...I saw how Danny kept looking at me...studying me with his piercing eyes. That could see inside you, and tell the future. Like he was...almost...afraid of me. Afraid of *me!* (*turns toward* DANNY, *pleadingly*) He stopped for gas and I got out of the car and with great dignity walked along a lane...in full view of Danny and the gas station attendant...my hair was kind of wild, I had sweated through my clothes, my hands were stained with something and there was something under my fingernails...but I hadn't *touched* those prissy little bastards, I didn't remember any blood or whatever Danny said, I wouldn't have done a fool thing like that with Danny breaking parole like he was and the car not registered in his name, I always had basic *survival sense.* So I walked away. Left my guitar behind. All trusting. Knowing that Danny could read my thoughts. Knowing that he would suddenly call me back. *Bobbie! Bobbie honey! You come back here this minute!* (*pause*) But he didn't. He just let me keep walking. (*in a slow mesmerized voice, strumming guitar*) And then...I found myself...at the edge of the continent. As far west as you can go without drowning. In Venice Beach I quickly made friends. They liked my music: I composed ballads one right after another to the asymmetrical primordial rhythms of the surf. Wild, they said, winking to one another, isn't he *wild,* isn't he something. Girls followed me around. Guys too—older men— Danny's age. Asking me for a lock of my hair. Love love love they tried to whisper but I had my counter-magic: hate hate hate. They pressed twenty-dollar bills into my hand—fifty-dollar bills—I lost track of how many. Later Melva did the same. In Lucky Pierre's where her boys brought her. And in the back seat of her big silver Rolls when I was her chauffeur...right on Westwood Boulevard in front of Helena Rubenstein where she'd had the full treatment ...three hours of it...while Bobbie the Monkey waited...in his chauffeur livery from the costume store. (MELVA *appears, fluffing her hair.*) Melva McLaren that was so hurt and furious when I didn't know who the hell she was—all those movie posters in her house, plastered on her bedroom walls—! (*pause*) Melva—always pretending she didn't want love at that particular moment! Oh not right now Bobbie oh not right *now* oh you beast. So I'd thrust my knuckles into her mouth—

(BOBBIE *stares at* MELVA, *as if in a trance. Then he turns away;* MELVA *turns aside.*)

BOBBIE: They all adored me...couldn't get enough of me...called me their furry little monkey...everyone except Danny.... (*furious, hurt*) Danny, you let me walk out of your life! Down a fucking road in Colorado! My heart was broken...you knew I couldn't live a day without you...you drove off and left me....

GARAGE ATTENDANT: (*approaches with guitar; amused*) This thing yours?

BOBBIE: (*taking it, slowly*) No note...no formal word of farewell.... Just...*nothing.*

(*Lights dim; darkness.*)

ACT TWO

SCENE ONE

Lights up. JUDGE *announces:* EL PORTAL: BOBBIE GOTTE-
SON'S FILM DEBUT. MELVA *in a long dress, high-heeled but
casual shoes, outsized sunglasses, bracelets. She is a former Holly-
wood actress who is still glamorous but at the same time somewhat
self-mocking. In* BOBBIE's *presence* MELVA *oscillates between arch
and almost desperate flirtatiousness, and a barely disguised revulsion.*

MELVA: I'm risking contempt of court...or extradition...whatever
they call it...but I can't possibly become involved in this case. If I
set foot on U.S. soil I will be served a subpoena. Anyway I don't
know anything about this latest maniac mass-murderer, nor do my
sons.

(BOBBIE *approaches, followed by* VLAD J. *with a hand-held camera.*
VLAD J. *wears tight-fitting jeans and a colorful T-shirt and sunglasses. He is barefoot.*)

MELVA: (*to audience, breathily*) We have survived scandal through the
decades but this Gotteson affair is the most—lewd. By far the most
lewd. (*to* BOBBIE) I'll just pretend you're not here. (*She mimes
jumping up on a stone wall, high above the sea.*) What madness it
was, Bobbie's debut on film, that first night! He never did grasp
the...magnitude of his talent...he kept hauling that silly guitar
everywhere...and it *did* frequently get in the way.

BOBBIE: Hey—what should I do? (*looking around, as if at an audience*)
What does she want me to do?

(VLAD J. *or an assistant takes* BOBBIE's *guitar from him.*)

Aren't I supposed to sing—?

MELVA: (*over her shoulder, airily*) I'll just pretend you're not here, you
little monkey!

BOBBIE: Miss McLaren, be careful—it's a long way down there—

MELVA: "Melva"!

BOBBIE: I mean Melva—Melva. (*He dances about, nervously.*) Hey Melva, am I supposed to—? With all these people around—?

MELVA: Ah, the air up here is so refreshing! A thousand feet above the ocean!

BOBBIE: (*jumps up beside her*) What if one of us falls?—what if you fall? Hey Melva you should wear more clothes, you should cover yourself up more—except your legs—your legs are nice for a woman your age—

MELVA: (*slaps him; then strokes his chin*) D'you see those?—those are hawks!—those are hawks circling up there—waiting for someone to fall onto the rocks—waiting for prey. What if they swoop down to get you? (*ruffling his hair*) What if they burrow in your hair like bats?

BOBBIE: (*beginning instinctively to play the game*) What if they burrow into *your* hair?

MELVA: (*looking around toward the* CAMERAMAN) How is this lighting? Is it too harsh?

BOBBIE: What's he doing following us!

MELVA: (*to* BOBBIE, *provocatively*) You ridiculous little furry monkey, you are so *slow*.

BOBBIE: That's never been said about Bobbie Gotteson before!

(MELVA *jumps off the wall and pulls* BOBBIE *after. In this scene it is difficult to tell—*BOBBIE *finds it difficult too—whether* MELVA *is sincere in her protestations, or merely acting. The sequence builds, however, to several seconds of abrupt violence, and the miming of a rape: after which, judging from* MELVA's *and* VLAD J.'s *response, we assume that this was the correct thing for* BOBBIE *to do, whether he is fully conscious of his actions or not.*)

MELVA: (*wrestling with* BOBBIE, *etc.*) Oh what are you doing, you diseased little— No you *don't*— I'm not one of your little-girl starlets! One of your sluts! I'm not someone you befriended on the beach! Stop! I'm famous! I don't need to be humiliated like this! Stop, that *hurts*—I said that *hurts*— You little bastard, I'll have you arrested—

BOBBIE: (*as if whispering*) Your face is slipping to one side. Your whole face—slipping.

MELVA: (*slapping at him*) Little wop bastard! Little monkey-bastard!

BOBBIE: I'm not a wop, I'm an American. I went to school in New Jersey. (*whispering*) Your mascara, your eyelashes—they're slipping to one side—don't you care?

MELVA: (*furiously, as* BOBBIE *straddles her*) I have sons your age—I'm above this sort of thing—you're hurting me—I'll have you arrested —put on Death Row—you're diseased, you're sub-human—I should never have brought you here—stop—my boys are watching —they've sneaked out here to watch—stop—wait—you're disgusting—I'm sick, I'm raw, I'm worn out—Bobbie—

(BOBBIE *strikes* MELVA *suddenly, to silence her. His behavior is brutal and ritualistic. Lights down.*)

VOICE: Oh Bobbie Bobbie Bobbie, you maniac!...what powers do you possess?

(*Lights up.* BOBBIE *comes forward with his guitar, smoothing down his hair, adjusting his clothing, etc.*)

BOBBIE: That was just the first of many nights at El Portal...where I made so many friends...so many powerful contacts. (*giggling*) I blacked out and when I woke up—I had a clump of blond hair in my fist, *hers*. And a bit of scalp and blood.

MELVA: (*in the distance*) You were needlessly rough! Uncouth!

BOBBIE: I tried to put it into music, the changes in my soul...I *think* I succeeded. That summer alone I wrote fifty songs...maybe one hundred. That song on the back of the Survivors' hit single last March, the one they called "Learning to Love"—that's my song— my name isn't in the credits but everybody knows. Those bastards stole my song and changed the title to that shitty unimaginative title—my song was called "Unlearning to Live" and was a beautiful song—I dedicated it to Melva—it was complex and subtle and demanding and disturbing and visionary and shattering—and much more—but those bastards, friends of Melva's son Curly, always zonked out of their heads on cocaine or whatever—they claimed they paid me $350 cash for the song, they had some kind of notarized paper to prove it, but it was a forgery—

MELVA: (*she has adjusted her clothing, combed her hair, etc., may be filing a broken fingernail with an emery board*) Bobbie, my precious boy, my brutal little Bobbie-glutton, wait until you get into show business! How proud I'll be, how the public will devour you! (*tussles his hair fondly*) My own boys are *such* a disappointment.... Oh here comes Vlad!

BOBBIE: Can I sing my own songs? Can I improvise? How big a stadium will you rent?

MELVA: Oh Bobbie you're so *droll*—every one of us has fallen in love with you!

(*Abrupt change of mood and pace. Scene has shifted to an unspecified interior.*)

VLAD J.: (*approaching* BOBBIE) Honey, let's swing right into a proposition we've all been meaning to make you, and now is the perfect time, let's explore the possibilities of a comedy series in which you play the role... the timely role, and I have the go-ahead from a very interested producer at the Studio, unfortunately not with us right now, but a quick telephone call would get him out here fast if he *knew*... who happened to be here. Anyway it's a really now idea and Melva balked because she has this mania for troubadours, I mean the funky gutsy strong stuff, but I'm going over Melva's head and take the chance and put the proposition to you, man, because I know you don't have an agent, don't believe in agents, but look here, honey, the idea some of us cooked up together was: a comedy series with you as the star's side-kick, the one who gets all the laughs or most of them, the one who sort of steals the scenes, you know, up until the last five minutes when things straighten out and the drama gets prepared for The End, but anyway you've got this incredible natural fantastic talent for being so goddam funny... I mean aside from your other talents... but this is going to be a family show, you know, on television. On television! And some of us thought, Jesus, it was almost a spontaneous group-thought, that I should do maybe a pilot while we're all together out here, like a family, pretty well-acquainted by now and not so self-conscious.

BOBBIE: A... comedy series? Television?

VLAD J.: Hey-y-y... Bobbie... Bobbie baby... baby Bobbie, honey.... Listen to me! I make enough in six weeks in television to finance

me the rest of the year, so I can do the kind of films I really want...
and the kind that is somehow in my nature... *my unique inexplic-
able nature* demanding to be given visual form.... And so, honey,
my proposition to you is—

BOBBIE: (*pushing* VLAD J. *violently away*) GET AWAY FROM ME!

(BOBBIE, *panting hysterically, runs from the room, into another
room where he hides under a bed.*)

MELVA: (*kneeling down to speak to* BOBBIE *under the bed*) Oh, Bobbie,
did he hurt your feelings...? Oh, Bobbie! Oh, Jesus, I told him to
let me talk to you. He's a Russian, he's never learned the nuances
of our language... don't pay any attention to him, Bobbie, please
come back out... please don't cry.... Everyone saw you run out of
the party and they're all very upset... you've upset them all,
Bobbie. None of us can stand to see you sad... to see anyone sad.
Everyone wants to see you perform, Bobbie... everyone's furious
with Vlad for upsetting you, and Vlad may just be out of a job if
they hear about this at the network. Bobbie? If I tell them you're
under the bed, nobody will believe me, Bobbie. You could make us
all so happy... and yourself so happy! *I*... if you'd just come back
out, honey, and show us how funny you are. There's no story-line
cooked up yet, for the comedy series, and they don't have a male
lead but it will be no trouble to find one—some tall blond clean-
faced boring kid, maybe a surfer, or a singer with a *good* voice—
and you, Bobbie, would be the scene-stealer! Did Vlad explain?
Honey please come back... let me wipe your face... that's my
good sweet Bobbie... yes... yes, crawl back out here. You've been
crying and your face is all dirty.

BOBBIE: Can I sing sometimes? Can I improvise?

MELVA: Oh sweet thing! (*kissing him*) We have all sorts of plans for
you!

(MELVA *leads* BOBBIE *across the stage; lights down.*)

SCENE TWO

Lights up. JUDGE *announces:* "17 MANNEQUINS AND A GUY":
BOBBIE GOTTESON'S FIRST SHORT FEATURE. *The film to*

*be shown in the courtroom is blurred out of all recognition. The
jurors react as if it were the grossest pornography.*

PROSECUTOR: (*with trembling voice*) And now that the courtroom has
been cleared—now—aren't you ready yet?—we are going to present one of the most repulsive and damning bits of evidence ever
offered by any prosecuting attorney in the history of—what is the
difficulty?—is something wrong with the projector?—in the history of justice itself in the State of California. Your honor, and
ladies and gentlemen of the jury, I hesitate even to read off the title
of this vile and indeed incredible piece of film footage— produced
for the illicit underground trade—shown at innumerable soirees
along the coast—fund-raising evenings for political hopefuls—
charity bazaars—$500-a-plate dinners: the notorious "17 Manne-
quins and a Guy" starring Bobbie Gotteson the defendant and 17
—you may count them—mannequins—dummies—*not* real women, thank God—though in a way it is all the more repulsive that
they were *not*—all the more bestial—unnatural— Can't you get
that thing to work? It was working perfectly last night— Your
Honor, and ladies and gentlemen of the jury, "17 Mannequins and
a Guy" was purchased by the District Attorney's office through a
series of secret negotiations with the director who shot it at El
Portal—a director of international reputation whose works have
won awards at film festivals everywhere, but whose name is missing
from the credits. In fact, there are no credits! For very good reasons,
as you will see. Not even the star, the maniac Bobbie Gotteson, is
given screen credit for his exhaustive, indefatigable performance—
ah, is it ready yet? No?—and the poor bastard claims he was never
paid. Such is the depraved state of contemporary culture that the
film's rental price soared from a paltry $1000 a night to the undis-
closed price the District Attorney's office paid, immediately after
Gotteson's arrest! Indeed, ladies and gentlemen of the jury, may we
not say—may we not hint—that contemporary culture itself is on
trial today. In this very courtroom? And what would be a just
verdict! And what would be a just sentence! Ah yes! Finally! Ladies
and gentlemen, the film runs for only eighteen minutes. One
minute for each of the dummies, and an 'arty' half-minute at the
start and finish. Though the film is hellish I must ask you *not* to
shut your eyes but to observe closely both the maniac's jack-
hammer-like sexual activity, and the deranged skill with which he
uses the machete—

(Film begins. Ad libs: "Oh, my God!" "It isn't possible—" "What's he doing...?" "Jesus Christ have mercy!")

PROSECUTOR: You'll note—here—at this point—how the defendant seemed to go into a trance—observe his eyes—no, his eyes—have you ever gazed upon anything more hideous? *(panting)* Obscene beyond our human ability to fathom... unparalleled in the history of.... The accused seemed to go into a trance, seemed to swing into a... what shall we call it?... a sword dance, a fertility-rite-mating-dance, so bizarre as to make us doubt our senses, and obscene beyond our human ability to fathom.... *(Film is shut off. He seizes the machete and swings it around with a surprising violence.)* You saw, ladies and gentlemen of the jury, how viciously the accused hacked that last mannequin to death—I mean, to pieces? You *saw*? You could not fail to see?

(Courtroom lights fade.)

BOBBIE: He could never use it the way I did. And neither could you! Or anyone else! *(pause)* Misunderstood as always. Misidentified with his physical being. As if Gotteson's secret was in his body! No, Gotteson made love to the spirit. He sang his melancholy-cheerful ballads to the spirit, in the ecstasy of his art. It was not his fault that a crass, craven society misappropriated him! Little girls not thirteen years old, pressing into his palm illicit pills, capsules, peyote buttons, reeking with excitement... young housewives... women like Melva... in fact, Melva's girl friends... crowding near... couldn't get enough of him....

MELVA: You hate me, don't you! You hate women, don't you! Believe me, Bobbie, you are *sick*.

BOBBIE: It wasn't my idea, dressing up as your chauffeur... parking on Westwood... the opium sodas... the screen test... the pilot film ... "17 Mannequins and a Guy." None of it was my idea, Melva.

MELVA: But you *were* a little glutton. You just ate it up, my plans for your career....

BOBBIE: *(softly)* But you did love me—?

MELVA: *(embarrassed)* Oh Bobbie—!

BOBBIE: Just a little? In the beginning? The first night at El Portal, when I was so naive? Or the first time you saw me in my chauffeur's livery? When you coaxed me out from under the bed, and kissed away my tears? When you came that night to post my bond and went pale at the sight of me, my poor battered face...?

MELVA: And when we got home, that very night, you tried to kill me! (*sighing*) Tried to strangle me.

BOBBIE: Why not?

MELVA: It was *discouraging*... how quickly you got like the others... like all men. At first so sweet and innocent and then... and then downhill.... Nasty, filthy.... More demanding.... And that wild day you and Irma did the machete dance! You frightened my boys so! It was wicked of Vlad to talk you into it—and poor Irma— stoned out of her skull for literally *days*—tempting you like that— *Do it to me Bobbie! Do it! Now!* And the others took up the chant *Sweet Bobbie and Irma, why not!* Oh Vlad was wicked—

BOBBIE: (*echoing her, half-smiling*) *Sweet Bobbie and Irma, why not?* —But I didn't, did I? With Irma?

MELVA: (*primly*) Of course not! We stopped you in time.

BOBBIE: (*clutching his head*) I was only playing around—joking. I remember that dance.

MELVA: You were *always* joking! Writing *I love you Melva* in your own blood on the kitchen wall.... It would have been so much fun to adopt you... the boys were heartbroken when I had to cancel our plans. I *did* love you, Bobbie. But you never loved me.

BOBBIE: (*uneasily*) I loved you, Melva! I loved Curly and Timothy too....

MELVA: No you didn't! (*pinching him*) When you found Timothy under our bed, that night in Mazatian you said he'd be the first to go—and you weren't joking.

BOBBIE: (*quickly*) I was joking. (*pause*) If only the screen test and the pilot film and the concert had come through.... If you hadn't all lied to me and laughed behind my back....

MELVA: Ah—it's always the same! As the wise old songwriters knew. You love someone who doesn't love you... he loves someone who doesn't love *him*... and so it goes. I could sense it that first night at Lucky Pierre's... all those beautiful young girls gazing soulfully at you...and you didn't care in the least, did you! You secretly hungered after older men. Like the Judge in this very Courtroom....

BOBBIE: (*sheepishly*) I suppose you're right.

MELVA: Older men. Gentlemanly men, but not *too* gentlemanly. Of a higher social class. Elegant but tough. Yes? Men who, if they happen to glance your way, can barely repress a fastidious shudder.

BOBBIE: (*offended*) Not *always!*

MELVA: (*turning to walk away*) Why anyone in her right mind...anyone of my stature...would fall in love with a motherfucker like you is...incomprehensible. A riddle.

BOBBIE: (*singing softly*) You love someone who doesn't love you...he loves someone who doesn't love *him*. (*smugly*) We call that *irony*.

(*Courtroom lights come up*.)

PROSECUTOR: (*wiping face; the film has ended*) Ladies and Gentlemen of the Jury...your Honor...I...I...hope you will allow these hellish images...to sink deeply into your hearts and souls...so that you can arrive at a clear unbiased judgment concerning our boy.

BOBBIE: But that wasn't me! I'm in my music, in my art! I'm pure spirit! *That wasn't me!* (*disdainfully*) I didn't kill them alone, either, but had disciples to help me. That actress Rosalind—she lied, she said she wasn't an actress—they all lied—she wasn't hallucinating when she saw three or four or five of me—she was correct. My disciples sprang out of my head. Not all of them were equipped with machetes—one of them was only a boy—he couldn't have held a machete much less swung it. He had a dimestore jackknife. That accounts for the confusion about weapons....

DEFENSE ATTY.: Bobbie, you're being most indiscreet! You're endangering our case—

BOBBIE: I'm not on trial! I can't be condemned to death! When I die it will be by a shutting-off from within.... I control my own fate. All death is suicide. *I control my own fate.* (*arrogantly*) THE TRIUMPH OF THE SPIDER MONKEY.

SCENE THREE

Lights up. JUDGE *announces:* THE FIRST OF THE VICTIMS:
LOUISE D. ON HER BIRTHDAY. BOBBIE *at door, ringing bell.*
He is dishevelled, high, manic; he is carrying a red box in which
the machete is hidden.

BOBBIE: Dance, dance, dance! Little Spider Monkey, dance for your
supper! Hand over hand up the drainpipe you climb— Defeating
the law of gravity—

LOUISE: (*in a bathrobe, just awakened*) Yes? Yes? Who is—?

BOBBIE: Hello! Good morning! Here I am! Am I too early? (*snapping*
fingers) Dance, dance—

LOUISE: (*staring*) Who are you? Do I know you?

BOBBIE: We all know each other out here! We were in the pool together
—eh? Bare and frolicking like fish and eels!

LOUISE: You mean...oh...that ridiculous party last Saturday.... I
don't really *know* those people....

BOBBIE: (*looking around room, snatches up magazine*) *This* is pretty
middle-class! Verging on the lower! I'm accustomed to high
living— You know me, Melva's adopted boy! How come you're
pretending you don't know me?— What's this, *Psychology Today*?
Hey Louise, you're not going to write me up, are you? Some kind
of case study or something?

LOUISE: (*confused, nervous; yet intrigued*) Oh—you're that friend of
Vlad's. Vlad and Sharleen. The musician—?

BOBBIE: Musician and composer and soon-to-be-TV-star.

LOUISE: I...I certainly didn't expect you to remember my name, or
where I live—

BOBBIE: Indelible memory! Never fails. (*taps forehead*) Even after my
fall...a fall of thirty-five feet. But I s'pose you know all about that?
Laughing behind my back, eh?

LOUISE: What?

BOBBIE: (*pacing about, picking things up and setting them down,*
sipping from a coffee cup) Ugh, that tastes like shit! It's stone-cold!

LOUISE: Oh, but— That's from last night, why don't you let me make you some fresh coffee?

BOBBIE: There isn't time! Isn't time!

LOUISE: I wish you had telephoned first—

BOBBIE: No money for a pay phone! Not a penny! Melva flew to Marrakech without saying goodbye! —Sharleen said, Hey Bobbie you'll adore Louise D., Louise was my Gestalt therapist in a dark time, brought me hope—maybe she can do the same for you. I kind of flashed on you that night: big tall gal: Big Sister Louise. You came on real strong with me, remember?

LOUISE: (*as if blushing*) I don't remember. I was probably playing around.

BOBBIE: Then you got all serious, talking with some—I don't know— lawyers or something—bitching about the government stopping some grant you had—mental health programs in the state—that kind of dreary shit—(*prancing about*) I don't believe in the State supporting all kinds of cripples and nuts and mental defectives... spastics... Mongoloid idiots....

LOUISE: (*laughing nervously*) Yes I do remember... you were so funny in the pool.

BOBBIE: (*holding out the box; then setting it beside him on the sofa where she can't reach it*) Hey—it's your birthday, eh? Present! Surprise!

LOUISE: What—? How did you know that?

BOBBIE: I don't know it, I just said it. (*pats the sofa beside him, but she keeps her distance*) I figured since I had a present.... *Is* it your birthday?

LOUISE: Yes.

BOBBIE: Well hell! The thought just flew into my mind.... Which birthday, Louise? Twenty-eight, twenty-nine...?

LOUISE: (*reluctantly*) Thirty.

BOBBIE: You came on real strong with me that night, didn't you? But I was drawn in another direction.

LOUISE: (*embarrassed*) Oh, well... I... I sometimes do foolish things...

I mean I consider foolish things. I was a little drunk. My work is so draining, and so depressing.... I have to have some relief....

BOBBIE: We all do! We all do!

LOUISE: *Would* you like me to make coffee? For both of us?

BOBBIE: No 'cause you'd leave the room, leave poor Bobbie all alone. (*pats sofa again, holds out arms*) Here I am, answering your summons! Your very own bridegroom! (*pause*) You *do* want to get married, don't you?

LOUISE: (*laughing*) You say such ridiculous things.... Let me make some coffee.

BOBBIE: Is there a phone out there?

LOUISE: Out—? In the kitchen—?

BOBBIE: Maybe the door locks. And you wouldn't come back. And I'd be all alone....

LOUISE: What are you talking about?

BOBBIE: You were one of them, weren't you? Laughing behind my back. Clapping, and smirking. Funny little Spider Monkey with a wiry scrunched-up tail inside his trousers....

LOUISE: Do you mean at the party? In the pool? I...I...I don't remember laughing.... I mean, not more than anyone else....

BOBBIE: You weren't ever an actress, were you? (*clutching at his head*)

LOUISE: An actress? Me? No—of course not. Maybe you've got me confused with....

BOBBIE: Are you lying? Are you reciting lines?

LOUISE: What's wrong with you?

BOBBIE: They had me crawl up a drain pipe at El Portal...while they were making the pilot-film...they were all high...maybe they knew the pipe was rusted.... I think you were there: weren't you there?

LOUISE: I'm not an actress...I'm Louise....

BOBBIE: I fell. I fell thirty-five feet. It's on film. It's on the record. I fell in slow motion while they screamed and tittered...I tried to grab onto some vines to save myself, but.... (*quickly*) I fell and injured the base of my spine and I will never be what you cunts call a *man* again.

LOUISE: (*shocked by his language*) You—say you hurt yourself? You fell—? Have you seen a doctor? My God, there's blood all over your arm....

BOBBIE: It's old blood. I never felt it. *Don't get alarmed.*

LOUISE: You *did* hurt yourself?

BOBBIE: Let's take a bubble bath together! Right now! Me and Melva— Me and Melva and the boys— (*dancing about*) What kind of bubble bath you got, Louise? Lavender and peach and spearmint and licorice! Let's wash off this smelly old distracting old blood. Then nobody'd know the difference.

LOUISE: (*with a peculiar smile*) You really *are*...something, aren't you.... Sharleen or was it Hans was telling me....

BOBBIE: In the bubble bath I'll unwrap the present! C'mon!

LOUISE: (*for a moment hesitating; then comes to her senses*) I know: I'll fix you some breakfast.

BOBBIE: No no *no*, not a step out of this room. Y'know why I came here, Louise? Last night I slept on the beach and your lovely bright eyes...your lovely eyes flashed to me out of the dark...and a voice said *Flee to Louise, she will help you, she's a finer person than the others etc., also her work with mental cases has made her charitable—and a little nuts herself.* And so—here I am. In the flesh. And it isn't absolutely certain, Louise honey, that the damage to the base of my spine is permanent. We—have—yet—to—determine—*that.*

LOUISE: You slept on the beach last night? Are you hungry? You seem light-headed. (*edging away*) Maybe I should fix you some breakfast—

BOBBIE: I don't eat! What the hell is this? (*jumping up*) Are you trying to defile me? Bobbie Gotteson doesn't require food like other people.... I'm spirit and energy, and if I look to you like a physical being (*runs his hands swiftly up and down his body, strokes his thighs*) that's your problem: your level of consciousness. Dance! Dance! Veils of illusions, veils of Maya! Universal applause! Now that I'm done with being a victim! Louise honey, I came to you because you have that big-sister look, I thought you were flashing me an important signal that night. So, here I am.

LOUISE: (*slowly*) But what do you want with me?

BOBBIE: What...do...I...want...with...you...? (*clutches at his head*) Oh, it's going to flash to me in a minute...!

LOUISE: Would you like a glass of milk? A drink? I have some—

BOBBIE: Bobbie Gotteson does not drink.

LOUISE: *Would* you like to wash up? I can get you clean towels, the tub is...the tub is clean.... (*no answer*) Would you like me to call a doctor?

BOBBIE: But I'm not the one who needs a doctor.

LOUISE: You're exhausted, you didn't sleep well last night, you've injured yourself.... Why don't you lie down here.... I can give you something to help you relax, to help you sleep....

BOBBIE: I don't sleep. The sun is my father. I take in energy without eating or sleeping. You might *think* the sun disappears like it was sleeping but actually it is always there but you can't see it.

LOUISE: (*trying to calm him, beginning to feel terror*) But it could be so pleasant, so wonderful, if you slept.... I could pull the blinds in here...you'd be perfectly quiet, and safe...you could stretch out.... I'll give you a very mild, very wonderful sedative I often take myself...I won't call a doctor if you don't want one...I won't call anyone....

BOBBIE: (*groggily, groping for the sofa, sitting down*) I...I did my best...I never claimed to be an actor, only a musician...composer.... Genius has to be...concentrated...you can't allow your talents to be fragmented.... My energies are flying out into the world *and I can't control them.*

LOUISE: (*gently*) Just let me get you the sedative, it's in my bathroom, in the medicine cabinet, I won't be gone a minute, I'm only stepping into the other room, why don't you relax, Bobbie, and stretch out there.... You'll be very comfortable there....

BOBBIE: You take a step toward that door and I'll slit your throat, Louise. It will happen so fast you won't *know* it, Louise! (*dreamily*) There isn't much time, Louise. There never is. Relationships don't develop. People ricochet off one another. I think it's tragic. I think it's sad. Without my guitar I'm deadly as a scorpion but that's not my fault like it's not the scorpion's fault. All I wanted, Louise, was to be a face on a billboard on the Strip!—was that too much to ask?

LOUISE: (*frightened*) I...I don't understand.... Please let me get you something to...to help you sleep....

BOBBIE: You're going to be one of my brides, Louise. I have so many—and I never wanted one—not a single one. You'll go down in history, Louise, as a bride of the Spider Monkey! But history doesn't last in California. I give us both six months.

LOUISE: (*beginning to cry*) Oh please let me help you.... Let me help you.... I don't want to die....

BOBBIE: Hey pal, you didn't want another birthday rolling around anyway, did you...!

(*The stage darkens.* LOUISE *falls to her knees.* BOBBIE *makes a gesture with the side of his hand as he stands above her. She topples over.*)

PROSECUTOR: And you struck down, in cold blood, that innocent girl!

BOBBIE: They were *all* innocent....

PROSECUTOR: And how can you possibly defend yourself, how can you hold your head up like a human being....

BOBBIE: A spider monkey.

PROSECUTOR: One of the most despicable creatures in the history of this office....

BOBBIE: But she didn't want another birthday rolling around, really! —she didn't. I read that out of the air. I had nothing personal against her. Both of us learned that morning that God is a maniac like me: anything you think of, He's thought of it first. You can't outdo him. Though you can try. My wildest song yet came to me in a rush-of-words *Hate hate hate hate hate hate* but then turned to *pity.* She'd done her fingernails the night before, *pity pity pity pity,* so I hacked her free of being female, I sent her soul spilling out of her body and back to God and the hell with it.

PROSECUTOR: Your Honor, I request that the accused's references to God be stricken from the record! This is...this is the most disgusting sort of blasphemy....

BOBBIE: But I meant to honor God! As one Maniac to another.... (*gavel*)

PROSECUTOR: To hint that God is an accomplice — God gives His permission — to foul creatures like yourself —

BOBBIE: But God is an artist too — not just a maniac — He does all sorts of things —

(BOBBIE *is restrained as the stage darkens.*)

SCENE FOUR

Lights up. JUDGE *announces:* THE EASTER SUNDAY MURDERS ON CHATEAU-GONTIER DRIVE.

ROSALIND: He just appeared — he came in through the back door — Barbara and Cyn weren't even up yet — it was eleven in the morning — Sunday — Easter Sunday — he came in through the back door and I knew from the first moment what — what — what would happen — because — because of his — eyes —

PROSECUTOR: And the man you are speaking of — ?

ROSALIND: Yes, there — Gotteson — of course — *him* — He walked in, the door was unlocked. Holly thought he was somebody's boy friend or maybe she was being, you know, flirtatious and cute, she was from Racine, Wisconsin and she thought you were supposed to act different out here so when this — when this man walked into the kitchen and asked us if we were actresses she said all kind of warm and bubbly and big eyed, Can I try my new yogurt-and-raisin-and-wheat-germ concoction out on you? — she was in her terrycloth beach robe — her hair all loose down her back — I walked in not knowing what was going on — who he was — and I looked at his face and I should have understood that this was a maniac.

BOBBIE: I was just asking a simple question! I wanted the answer to a simple question! (*gavel*)

ROSALIND: Then Annie came in — and Suzanne — And — (*pauses, agitated*) it happened the way I've told you so many times.

PROSECUTOR: But you must explain to the Court — to his Honor, and to the Ladies and Gentlemen of the Jury.... (*no response*) Surely you want the loathsome creature who hacked your roommates to death to receive the justice that is his due?

ROSALIND: (*softly*) But there were more than one....

PROSECUTOR: (*annoyed*) Now we've been all through that, haven't we! You agreed that Gotteson's 'helpers' were invisible, and that they must have been hallucinations—

ROSALIND: (*slowly*) Hallucinations. Yes. There was only one murderer ...one main murderer...who is sitting...here...in this Court-room.

PROSECUTOR: Would you point him out?

ROSALIND: (*points at* BOBBIE, *averting her face*) I got out of the kitchen. I knew something was going to happen. He must have left the... the machete out on the porch...but I knew...I knew from his eyes...something was wrong. My girl friends were joking with him, they thought he was...well you know...they—thought— he—was—*cute*.

PROSECUTOR: (*incredulous*) Your girl friends thought the maniac Bobbie Gotteson was—*cute*?

ROSALIND: (*quickly*) He has a sort of immediate appeal...his smile, and his eyes...he smelled of bubble bath...I mean, he said that's what it was...licorice bubble bath. But then...well he was obvi-ously *high*...and angry about something...he kept saying we were actresses, weren't we, friends of Vlad J.'s...and we told him we weren't, we had all kinds of different jobs. He asked if we knew who Vlad J. was and Barbara came in half-dressed and yawning and said oh sure she knew him—a Russian or something—a famous film director—she didn't *know* him but had met him once or twice at parties. And then.... (*distressed*) I shouldn't have left them. But.... But I knew that something was going to.... But I should have run outside.... Or gone upstairs and locked the door and telephoned the police. But.... But I didn't know.... I mean, I'm always imagining things, my friends laugh at me, I'm from Detroit, I'm not always...trusting...about strangers. (*pause*) So I, I didn't go upstairs...I stayed in the living room...I couldn't decide what to do...and then it was too late: then it started. He— they—he—it started, in the kitchen—there was so much scream-ing—and he chased Cyn into the living room—he had the machete —I was hiding behind the sofa—

BOBBIE: Hiding behind the sofa! But I looked behind the sofa!

ROSALIND: I couldn't believe it was happening. I could see these feet...
these shapes...bounding everywhere in the room, four or five of
them...one of them was a little boy with a jack-knife...but, no, I
didn't really see them...just feet and legs...and then...bodies...
the girls when they fell. There was a great deal of blood. There was
a great deal of confusion. I'm not sure it really happened.... How
could it have happened...? (*pause*) And then he ran into Joan's
and Cyn's bedroom and rummaged around...there was only one
of him now...and then he came back. He was wearing Joan's
white bellbottom trousers and a red shirt and I think he was barefoot. There was only one of him but he was talking to himself. I
was terrified that he would find me. That he would...peek under
the sofa and see me. And smile. And.... But he didn't. He left—he
left by the back door—and it was all over.

PROSECUTOR: (*deeply moved, or pretending to be so*) Your Honor...
Ladies and Gentlemen of the Jury...having listened to this distraught young woman's testimony...you...you can certainly see
how...how *serious* this all is.

ROSALIND: (*helped down from the stand*) And yet I never felt—even
when the slaughter was taking place—that there was anything
personal about it. That he meant—you know—any personal
harm.

(*Courtroom darkens.*)

BOBBIE: (*sheepishly; defiantly*) ...And after that people didn't like me
any more. Every door was shut against me.

SCENE FIVE

Lights up. JUDGE *announces:* THE REDEMPTION OF THE
SPIDER MONKEY. *Headlines are shown, or read by various
actors.* BOBBIE'*s voice rises behind theirs.*

ESCAPED KILLER AT LARGE
POLICE SEARCH FOR MACHETE MANIAC
8TH YOUNG WOMAN FOUND DEAD

ESCAPE IN BROAD DAYLIGHT

PASSERSBY DO NOTHING
TO HALT FLEEING
MACHETE MURDERER

THE CURE FOR STAMMERING

MANIAC STRIKES AGAIN

BOBBIE: As finger-sized fish float in the harbor
belly-up and harmless
so we float in one another's lives
meaning no harm
and no one is to blame
for that immense single triumph
in which we all float belly-up
innocent
and terrible

(BOBBIE, *cheeks rouged, dressed in an ill-fitting black suit, becomes visible.*)

BOBBIE: (*indicating rouge*) A contemptible job they did of it, the State's cosmeticians! I never wore rouge, in life. Maybe a little lipstick... Melva's Bruised Plum... which was so wickedly and lasciviously dark... and tasted like a real plum; and one night she brushed some of her jet-black waterproof mascara on my eyelashes... while admitting that I hardly needed mascara, my lashes were so thick. (*viciously*) That cunt Melva! Why didn't I.... (*wriggles his fingers*)

PROSECUTOR: What none of us can understand, Bobbie, is your... curious attachment to the last of your grisly victims, Doreen B. We can understand, we can certainly understand, every wild sickening unspeakable thing you've done, indeed we are craving to hear even more—but we find it *very* difficult to understand your...sentiment.

BOBBIE: The cure for stammering...the cure for any compulsion....

PROSECUTOR: Surely you didn't fall in love with her? That last pathetic little girl....

BOBBIE: After the second fiasco...after I was forced to flee in 'broad daylight'...carrying the machete carelessly wrapped in a skirt... after witnesses got a clear look at me...and I made a complete fool of myself... after that terrible morning... I had to hide out in utter solitude to address a serious question to myself: *Which direction was my life headed in?*

PROSECUTOR: And so, Bobbie, in your activities as a killer you followed the same basic pattern of promiscuity begun so many years ago, as a boy in Juvenile Detention...? Through you, or boys just like you, diseases are spread across the continent. There is an epidemic of diseases, isn't there? What we are asking you, Bobbie, is just this: to the best of your knowledge is it possible that you are only a pawn?—a tool?—that you and diseased boys like you are actually being used by intelligent forces to infect the American continent with debilitating and brain-rotting diseases...?

BOBBIE: No.

PROSECUTOR: But it is a possibility, isn't it? We find it remarkable that someone as degenerate as yourself, as mentally deficient as our records show you to be and your dull-eyed appearance argues you actually are, can answer that question so confidently!

BOBBIE: (*to himself, and us, no longer on the stand*) Throughout my life I did worry about that—about influences. About the way the moon acted upon the ocean, and how it might act upon me. After the stormy session in Louise's house, when I must have blacked out for ten, or maybe fifteen minutes, and just seemed to fall through the floor and keep on falling, and thrashing around, arms and legs, hacking and plunging and gasping for breath, oh sweet Jesus I had to take stock of myself. I was frightened. These recent events, the Machete leaping to such life—because the Machete had sliced up more women than the State's records attest—the Machete sweeping and plunging and pulsating and throbbing in a way the guitar had not, this frightened me because my soul blacked out and abandoned me to whatever was going on. I stood under the cold freezing shower and thought of penance. Getting my mind straight and reason-driven, Bobbie Gotteson in his own head again, not running wild. I thought of how one of my buddies at Terminal Island had explained to me how a kindly teacher of his once taught him to conquer his stammering: *by making himself stammer on purpose.* (DOREEN B. *appears: beautiful, in her late teens, looking strangely like* BOBBIE.) I was wandering in Hermosa Beach... 1 A.M.... found myself in a TacoBurger Palace... and she (*indicating* DOREEN) was on duty... sweet little-girl waitress....

DOREEN B.: (*in a slow, dream-like, ethereal voice*) What would you like...?

BOBBIE: (*reading, with some difficulty, from a newspaper*) "WIT-NESSES DISAGREE ON MACHETE MURDERER'S DESCRIP-TION...."

DOREEN B.: Sorry—what? I beg your....

BOBBIE: No clues in this paper! Nothing substantial! Someone said I was tall and someone said I had a limp—do I have a limp?—a woman said I was a *Mexican*—and someone else said—what was it?—"a short stocky barrel-chested fellow with a tattoo on his right forearm"— (*gazing at* DOREEN B., *smiling*) The last of my brides! I've come so far....

DOREEN B.: (*after a pause; in the same dream-like manner*) What would you like...? It's getting late, we're about to close.

BOBBIE: (*looking around, helplessly*) There's nothing I want. I'm starving but I can't eat. The sun is my father, I can't eat...human food.

DOREEN B.: Don't you have any money? If you're starving....

MANAGER: (*from far away*) Doreen, do you want a ride home? I'm closing up now....

BOBBIE: (*indicating newspaper*) Next-door neighbors heard these poor actresses screaming for help but nobody came to help! Can you imagine! And this Louise D., the other one, have you read about *her?*—her next-door neighbor turned his television set on full blast and didn't hear a *thing*—it's all reported here. A sickening... depressing...newspaper. (*to* DOREEN B., *taking her arm, as they walk to the side*) Are you—taking pity on me? Is that why you're looking at me like that?

DOREEN B.: If you don't have any money, if you're actually starving, I could maybe...I mean...he's closing up here but....

BOBBIE: (*speaking half-angrily to the Court*) Her look went through me like a blade! It was sheer animal pity, she couldn't help herself, because by then I was already dying....

PROSECUTOR: (*contemptuously*) Well—get on with it! Don't embroider! We all know you killed this one too, no matter how you've been babbling and snuffling all these months—claiming she was so special. It's typical of a mass murderer to be florid and sentimental. (*mimicking* BOBBIE) Because her name was Doreen! Because she took pity on you! Because she was a beautiful little girl and so *very* innocent.

DOREEN B.: Where do you come from? You're not from around here, are you?

BOBBIE: Where is this? Where—exactly—is—this—

DOREEN B.: You look like my brother. When you first walked in the place I thought—

BOBBIE: Brother? What brother?

DOREEN B.: My mother couldn't keep him, she had to give him up, I last saw him when he was maybe four, five years old— His eyes— his hair—the way you smile—

BOBBIE: The cure for stammering!—it's to make yourself do something you don't actually want to do, so that you won't do it in the future —or ever again. To do something—you don't want to do—so that you *won't* do it—ever—again.

DOREEN B.: You're not from around here, are you? I'm not either—I'm from all the way back East—I live alone here—do you live alone? —where did you come from tonight? As soon as you opened the door and—

BOBBIE: (*thoughtfully*) Well—I couldn't have come from anything normal and good. Because if I came from anything normal and good I would *be* normal and good, wouldn't I? I couldn't be Bobbie Gotteson, which I have spent my whole life being.

DOREEN B.: (*laughing, uncomprehending*) You talk so funny! You talk so *serious.* . . .

BOBBIE: Now listen: if everything in the world comes from the world, or from someplace called the world, well then, and the world is normal and good (which it would have to be, wouldn't it?) . . . normal and good . . . well . . . I might be normal and good after all. Unless I'm not Bobbie Gotteson. I might not . . . *be* . . . here at all.

DOREEN B.: You're hungry and tired. . . .

BOBBIE: I don't know where I came from! It couldn't have been the sun . . . I don't know. . . . Or why you took me home with you, Doreen. I wasn't your brother.

DOREEN B.: Your eyes—your hair—your voice—

BOBBIE: Stop looking at me! I didn't ask for this! (*He mimes her murder.*) My only bride. . . . (*He cradles her body.*) I tried to explain to her. My whole life came to that—explaining to *her*. That maybe —maybe—I wasn't there at all. I didn't exist. I don't exist. After my death I left my brain to the Neuropsychiatric Department of the Medical Institute of Los Angeles and my body-parts to the souvenir hunters and there was something there, there *was* something there, so evidently I did exist. But I don't know where I came from. Or why you were so kind to me, Doreen.

DOREEN B.: Why—?

BOBBIE: The voice *hate hate hate* . . . the voice . . . but I couldn't hear it this time . . . it was too faint. . . . Doreen, maybe it wasn't me! Did you happen to see . . . is there someone else in this room . . . with a long scroungy wiry tail. . . .

DOREEN B.: Oh, don't leave me . . . something has happened to me . . . I'm afraid. . . .

BOBBIE: I can't hear it! Any of the voices! *Hate hate hate* . . . *pity* . . . Danny and Melva and Vlad J. and the actresses and Louise D. though she tried too clumsily to trick me . . . as if anyone could trick *me*. . . . (*to* DOREEN B., *shaking her*) Don't die! Don't leave me! You're the one who can't leave me! (*pause*) My heartbeat is slowing, like yours. I can feel it. I am bleeding to death. . . . Doreen— what a sweet name! Why did you take pity on me, why did you bring me here, all the way to the Pacific Coast! It's too *far*—the distances are horrible. Doreen—

DOREEN B.: I'm beginning to see. . . . I can look over. . . . I can see over the edge. . . .

BOBBIE: Don't leave me! Wait—

DOREEN B.: I can see over the edge, it isn't far. . . .

BOBBIE: No! Wait! You can't leave me like the rest of them!

DOREEN B.: I'm not leaving you. . . . (*dies*)

BOBBIE: But what is it like! What were you saying!—I don't want to be left alone here, I'm afraid, there's all this—blood—and the dark— (*weakly*) Hate hate hate . . . hate. . . . She betrayed me, I wanted to hate her, but . . . I was too weak . . . I had lost too much blood. . . .

Doreen—am I there with you? Am I there? You feel so *heavy*—

PROSECUTOR: Ladies and gentlemen of the jury, you *must* resist Bobbie's shameless appeal for your sympathy. It may have happened just as he says—he has never, so far as we know, lied—it's a condition of his madness—but you must keep your distance—you must remember that he has always been devilishly seductive despite his monkey-ugly looks....

JURORS: (*scattered voices*) But—isn't it *sad!* It's heartbreaking, actually —that's what it is—*heartbreaking*. Why, he's falling in love at the very end of his life.

But it's so morbid! It's much *too* morbid, even if it did happen that way!

Now now now—look here: I wouldn't be taken in by all this. Once a fag always a fag, you know.

Gays they call themselves now. *Gays*. Not *fags!*

Isn't it touching! And the girl is so pretty!

It *is* touching! I'm crying like a baby....

A cheap fag trick to enlist our sympathies....

But Bobbie is crying too! Look, Bobbie is crying too!

PROSECUTOR: Yes, the little monkey was always devious. It accounts for his posthumous success. And his corpse *is* rather attractive—if you like the troubadour type.

(VOICES, PROSECUTOR, *Court fade.*)

BOBBIE: (*to* DOREEN B.'s *limp form*) What is death, is it a place?—a feeling?—is it dark?—is it light?—is it like the ocean?—or the sun?—the desert?—the locker?— Is it pitch-black with just your heart beating and then it *isn't* beating—Do you forgive me, Doreen? Do you love me? My bride— I never *saw* a dead person before. (*pause*) Whose blood is this? (*pause*) Why is it so quiet! The world must have ended.... The second after it ends, *this* is how it will sound: so quiet.... None of us left.... Nothing to be heard....

(*pause*) Doreen, I know you can hear me. I know you're listening. You've made yourself so heavy but I know you're listening and I know you forgive me. Doreen—every song I wrote was for you. It was just a way of trying to hide something so sad it can't be said —except for music— Doreen, I *wasn't* your brother—how could a monkey be your brother! (*stands*) Gotteson sticky with blood—it's always the same—sweating and stinking—sticky with blood— trapped in his body—Gotteson the Spider Monkey—in the locker —in Rahway Correctional—in the hospital—in the morgue—in court—in Doreen's bed—performing for the inmates—Spider-Monkey-Climbing-Up-a-Pole!—performing for the inmates—isn't he darling!—isn't he gifted!—those eyelashes!—that tail!—Gotteson Inside—Gotteson Outside—all's one Gotteson—unrepeatable—(*abortive running movements, into the street*) Where is it? The ambulance? Hasn't anyone called the ambulance? Why is it taking so long? Where are they? Where are you all—hiding? (*increasingly agitated, though not shouting*) I said call an ambulance! It isn't too late! Do something! Help me! It isn't too late! Bastards! Where are you all hiding . . . ?